HIDDEN ALLEYWAYS *of* WASHINGTON, DC

Hidden Alleyways

of WASHINGTON, DC

A History

KIM PROTHRO WILLIAMS

Georgetown University Press / *Washington, DC*

Library of Congress Cataloging-in-Publication Data

Names: Williams, Kimberly Prothro, 1962– author.
Title: Hidden alleyways of Washington, DC : a history / Kim Prothro Williams.
Description: Washington, DC : Georgetown University Press, [2023] | Includes bibliographical references and index.
Identifiers: LCCN 2023001170 (print) | LCCN 2023001171 (ebook) | ISBN 9781647123925 (hardcover) | ISBN 9781647123932 (ebook)
Subjects: LCSH: Alleys—Washington (D.C.)—History. | Washington (D.C.)—History. | Washington (D.C.)—Social conditions.
Classification: LCC F203.7.A1 W55 2023 (print) | LCC F203.7.A1 (ebook) | DDC 975.3—dc23/eng/20230126
LC record available at https://lccn.loc.gov/2023001170
LC ebook record available at https://lccn.loc.gov/2023001171

This paper meets the requirements of ANSI/NISO Z39.48-1992 (Permanence of Paper).

24 23   9 8 7 6 5 4 3 2 First printing

Printed in the United States of America

Cover design and interior design by Erin Kirk

Generous support for this project was provided by Furthermore: a program of the J. M. Kaplan Fund.

Furthermore:
a program of the J.M. Kaplan Fund

Other Titles of Interest from Georgetown University Press

Between Freedom and Equality: The History of an African American Family in Washington, DC
    Barbara Boyle Torrey and Clara Myrick Green

Black Georgetown Remembered: A History of Its Black Community from the Founding of
"The Town of George" in 1751 to the Present Day; 30th Anniversary Edition
    Kathleen Menzie Lesko, Valerie M. Babb, and Carroll R. Gibbs

A Georgetown Life: The Reminiscences of Britannia Wellington Peter Kennon of Tudor Place
    Grant S. Quertermous, Editor

George Washington's Final Battle: The Epic Struggle to Build a Capital City and a Nation
    Robert P. Watson

Sixteenth Street NW: Washington, DC's Avenue of Ambitions
    John DeFerrari and Douglas Peter Sefton

Spy Sites of Washington, DC: A Guide to the Capital Region's Secret History
    Robert Wallace and H. Keith Melton with Henry R. Schlesinger

CONTENTS

ACKNOWLEDGMENTS

Many individuals have contributed to and encouraged this publication. I am most indebted to David Maloney, Steve Callcott, Amanda Molson, Kim Elliott, and many of my other colleagues and former colleagues in the District of Columbia's State Historic Preservation Office who, in response to development pressures that were beginning to infiltrate the interiors of DC's large city squares, saw the need to identify and research the history of the city's alleys and their buildings. This desire to have more knowledge to guide development in our historic neighborhoods propelled me to undertake a study—the DC Historic Alley Buildings Survey—which in turn has led to additional research and this publication. The research and recordation project of over two thousand historic alley buildings within the original city limits took three years and an enthusiastic group of students, interns, and volunteers, including Namon Freeman, Courtney Ball, Clare Eberle, Lauren McHale, Audrey Stefenson, Nick Efron, Renan Snowden, Mollie Hutchings, Christine Huhn, and Jacqueline Drayer. These dedicated people spent countless hours walking the city's alleyways collecting data, conducting research, and entering the findings into a database for analysis. They brought great energy to the project, even as the number of one-story garages needing to be recorded heavily outstripped the number of more architecturally intriguing alley buildings. I greatly appreciate the time and commitment of all of those who participated in the survey effort.

I am grateful to the many DC residents, neighborhood organizers, local historians, planners, architects, and academicians who greeted the study with interest and encouraged me to "write a book." A huge thanks to those neighborhood leaders who organized speaking events, especially to Nicki Cymrot of the Hill Center, Faye Armstrong of Historic Mount Pleasant, Rebecca Miller of the DC Preservation League, and Rick Bush of the Dupont Circle Conservancy, who hosted events for me and brought in the crowds. I am especially appreciative of the support of Naylor Court resident David Salter, who championed my work and shared his own research findings with me, and of historian Matthew Gilmore, who showcased my research on alley buildings at a DC history conference in pre-COVID times. I am grateful to Chris Myers Asch and

Jane Levey for working with me to publish an article, "The Surviving Cultural Landscape of Washington's Alleys," in the journal *Washington History* in 2015.

I wish to extend a big thanks to the many archivists and librarians in DC who helped me locate and secure images to illustrate the book. A special thanks goes out to everyone at the DC History Center, especially research services librarian Jessica Smith and librarian Derek Gray at the People's Archive at the Martin Luther King Jr. Memorial Library.

This book could not have been accomplished, though, without my friends and colleagues in the DC history community who encouraged me to take the research to the next level and pursue a book. Don Hawkins, John de Ferrari, and Peter Sefton were the principal instigators, and John and Peter further introduced me to Georgetown University Press editor Don Jacobs, who embraced the idea of such a book and converted the vision into reality.

I am truly grateful to my readers, Mara Cherkasky, who read the first chapters early on and offered invaluable advice for moving forward, and to John de Ferrari and Jane Levey, who read the manuscript for Georgetown University Press with critical eyes and worked with me in the process to reorganize and tighten chapters. And then they turned around and did it again with the revised draft. I am truly indebted to both of them.

Finally, a big thanks to my friends and family who have endured listening to me talk about historic alleys for some time now! A special heartfelt thanks to my husband, Richard, who has been a longtime fan of the topic and my talking about it. As my own interest in the subject waned at times during the process, Richard's unending fascination propelled me along and convinced me that others would be equally intrigued. I hope he's right!

HIDDEN ALLEYWAYS *of* WASHINGTON, DC

Introduction

This is a book about Washington's historic alleys—alleys as inhabited spaces for people and animals, as places of commerce and industry, and as refuges for artists, artisans, and craftspersons seeking affordable space and artistic community in a growing city. It is a story of the physical history of the alleys, from their initial manifestation on paper in the Plan of the City of Washington in the late eighteenth century to places of abode for enslaved African Americans escaping bondage or for newly freed Blacks and immigrants seeking new life in the nation's capital. It is a social history of humanitarians and urban reformers aspiring to eradicate the alleys and alley dwellings to rid the city of its slums but with no concrete plan for housing those residents being displaced. It is a story of entrepreneurs who built businesses in the alleys, converting them from secondary byways to commercial and industrial centers that teemed with workers and machinery providing services and consumer goods to a growing city. And it is about refuge and opportunity away from the pressures of city life.

But mostly it is about the physical remnants of a city celebrated more for its grand plan, its public squares and circles, and its monumental government buildings and exuberant rowhouse neighborhoods than for its concealed inner blocks. The surviving alley buildings—from modest dwellings to stables and workshops, studios, and garages—are but a small percentage of those that once occupied the city's alleys. As economic and social trends reduced the functional necessity of alley buildings over time, they have become increasingly rare and obsolete—like the impossibly small, single-horse stable built around 1885 that still stands at the rear of a Capitol Hill rowhouse.

While these buildings survive to tell the story of the past, they also risk obscuring it as they are repurposed for wholly different uses and for an entirely different segment of the population than those of their origins. Alley dwellings that once sheltered the most indigent of the city's population are now home to some of its wealthier residents; stables that once housed horses and hay now serve as trendy cafés and fine-dining restaurants; bakeries and bottling plants, once sources of the city's service economy, now form the base of high-rise steel-and-glass condominium buildings or provide retail space for high-end designer commodities accessible only to the few.

Though few survive today, one-story horse stables like this one from 1885, located in the alley behind the 300 block of A Street NE on Capitol Hill, were once common features in the city's alleys. Two-story stables survive in greater quantity, though, and many are being repurposed as residential and retail spaces. (Photo by author, 2021.)

This book recalls the history of the city's alleys and alley buildings as they are undergoing a major period of transformation. It draws on years of research and site work that I conducted both in my capacity as an architectural historian at the District of Columbia's State Historic Preservation Office (SHPO) and independently. The SHPO study—the DC Historic Alley Buildings Survey—is an architectural survey of historic alley buildings within the boundaries of the original L'Enfant Plan city and Georgetown and undertaken to support historic preservation and redevelopment efforts. In 2011–13 student interns and volunteers walked the city's alleys to identify historic alley buildings more than fifty years old, researched and recorded basic information on their original uses and dates of construction, and then developed a historical context for understanding and evaluating the identified buildings. This survey provided, for the first time, a comprehensive database of historic alley buildings citywide and a contextual understanding of their historical value. Today many of the city's alleys and their alley buildings are celebrated as an important cultural landscape and distinctive urban space that contribute to a vibrant social realm. At the same time, this revitalization of the alleys has obscured what came before. This book is a reminder of that past.

The DC Alley Museum is an outdoor collection of public art murals painted on several buildings in Blagden Alley NW. Since 2015 this artwork, made possible by the DC Commission on the Arts and Humanities, has contributed to a vibrant urban realm in the alley. The *LOVE* mural, shown here, fills the first-story openings in a row of buildings constructed in 1885 as dwellings but later converted into garages. (Mural by Lisa Marie Studio; photo by author, 2021.)

Hidden Alleyways of Washington, DC is divided into seven chapters that discuss the physical and social history of the District's alleys. The book draws on a host of primary and secondary sources for information, from historical survey plats and maps to city directories, newspaper articles, and government reports to published articles and books. For the social history of the inhabited alleys, the book relies heavily on the work of social historian and author James Borchert, whose many articles and published book, *Alley Life in Washington: Family, Community, Religion, and Folklife in the City, 1850–1970*, form the basis of our understanding of the social structure of alley life.

Chapter 1, "The Origins of DC's Alleys," provides an overview of Washington's unique system of alleys as originally platted and how they came to be inhabited. Chapter 2, "Alley Life," paints an overview of the socioeconomic composition of the alleys, the challenges alley residents faced, and the communities they built to overcome those challenges. Chapter 3, "Humanitarian Reform Efforts," outlines the decades-long attempts by housing reformers, humanitarians, politicians, and civic leaders to eradicate alley dwellings and the city's inhabited alleys in the name of aesthetics and the belief that poor environments contributed to antisocial behavior and poverty. Chapter 4, "Twentieth-Century Alley Renovation," addresses the mid-twentieth-century movement to renovate alley dwellings in the years before they were to be demolished by final decree according to the Alley Dwelling Act of 1934—legislation intended to eradicate inhabited alleys and alley dwellings in the city. This chapter focuses on the social impact of that movement as the owners of deteriorated alley dwellings displaced the longtime, mostly Black residents and instead of demolishing the dwellings as required, upgraded and improved them for sale or rent to higher-income, White professionals. Chapter 5, "Commerce and Industry in the Alleys," illustrates the multiuse nature of the alleys and the rise of manufacturing and other businesses that took root in them to accommodate the needs of the growing city. Chapter 6, "Washington's Bohemia," describes the alleys as emerging artistic communities in the late nineteenth and early twentieth centuries as artists and craftspersons built studio buildings and repurposed former horse stables and carriage houses for their studios and communal live-work spaces. Chapter 7, "Reimagining Alleys," focuses on recent development projects that are "reinventing" the city's alleys and contributing to both urban revitalization and gentrification of the city's historic downtown neighborhoods.

The city's alleys were never intended to be seen. They were deliberately hidden from public view to conceal the people and services behind the grand design envisioned by Washington's early planners. But as their story emerges here from those shadows, it brings to light the good and ill of the history of our nation's capital, while introducing a new dimension to the increasingly dense and complex city.

CHAPTER I

The Origins of DC's Alleys

ALLEYS ARE VISUALLY APPEALING and socially alluring spaces. The word alone conjures up the old-world charm of labyrinthine side streets with a maze of cafés and shops, such as those behind the canals of Venice, in the souks of Morocco, and in the covered bazaars of Istanbul. These narrow passageways and their small-scale buildings create a humanizing and pedestrian-friendly atmosphere. Unlike these meandering old-world alleys, the alleys of most American cities cut directly through their urban blocks, mainly as a means of access to garages and for municipal services such as trash pickup. The alleys of the original city of Washington, DC, however, are more like their old-world counterparts, full of people and life.

Washington's alleys are not singular routes that cut in a linear fashion through the city, one block after another. They are instead a series of connecting arms and legs within city blocks (known as "squares" in DC) that form distinct networks. On paper, the alleys, with their various and narrow appendages at the center of the squares, offered an informality to the grand and formal L'Enfant Plan, with its wide streets and diagonal avenues.

In life, too, the alleys presented a glaring paradox to the growing prosperity and planned architectural beauty of the nation's capital. Deep within the center of the city's blocks and shielded from the public streets, these alleys were crammed with people and an assortment of buildings—namely, rudimentary alley dwellings housing the city's poorest inhabitants. Throughout the decades and unlike other American cities, Washington's alleys were inhabited spaces where the poorest of its residents formed insular communities distinct from the outside world. The history of Washington's alleys is a story of physical contrasts and human perseverance. And most recently it is one of rediscovery and of reimagining that, for good or ill, leaves the memory of the people and past behind.

Alley Origins

Though it comes in many configurations and forms, an alley is essentially a narrow street or passage behind a principal artery. Its origins can be traced to ancient Greek town planning and the establishment

This map detail, showing an area east of the US Capitol, highlights the current configuration of alleys in this part of Capitol Hill. Although many original alley layouts have been altered over time, many, like the readily recognizable *H*- and *I*-shaped ones in this map, are still apparent. These alleys, referred to as "blind" or "hidden" alleys as they were concealed from public view, historically housed thousands of low-income residents. (DC Office of Planning, 2021.)

of the urban grid. For thousands of years, this grid system heavily influenced the layout of new cities and towns in Europe and America.

Upon coming to the New World in 1681, William Penn laid out his plan for Philadelphia according to a large and formal ancient grid that was inspired by the plans for rebuilding London after the Great Fire of 1666. Penn had been in London during the fire and was witness to the problems of irregular, crowded streets of the medieval city. So, for Philadelphia—the first British colonial city to be designed according to a formal master plan—Penn planned a system of large blocks formed by straight, wide, tree-lined streets to avoid the filth, disease, and fires that devastated London. As designed, Penn's plan did not contain alleys, but within the first two decades of its existence, as the city developed from the Delaware River to the Schuylkill, smaller lanes and alleys were created through the large blocks to provide more direct access to the centers of commerce. Eventually tiny houses arose along these lanes, later called "little" or "minor" streets, providing homes for the working class. One was Elfreth's Alley, which had emerged in 1703 as a cart path for tradespersons seeking to carry their goods through the crowded city to the port.

As Americans moved south and west in the eighteenth and early nineteenth centuries, many of their new towns copied the basic grid formula and, for the first time, introduced alleys from the outset into the city blocks. In 1830 all fifty-eight blocks making up the original city of Chicago included sixteen-foot alleys running through the center of them. In Galveston, Texas, alleys were a feature of its original 1838 city plan,

Ancient Alley Origins

In 466 BCE, with the rebuilding of Miletus in Asia Minor, proto–city planners had the opportunity to lay out an entire urban center in deliberate and uniform fashion. The result, often attributed to Hippodamus—a Greek architect and native of Miletus—was a regular grid system of streets aligned orthogonally and enclosing large rectangular blocks. Based on archeological evidence, it appears that a system of minor streets and alleys evolved in the gridded city to provide quicker passage for pedestrians. Several decades later, alleys four and a half feet wide divided the large city blocks of the new city of Olynthus in Macedonia. These alleys, planned along with the streets as original elements of the town, are the first known "designed" alleys.

intended as much to service the rear of the houses facing the main streets as to confine the enslaved population to the enslavers' land. While the precise forms and names of alleys varied from the "minor streets" of Baltimore to the "back streets" of New Orleans to the "blind alleys" of Washington, DC, they all came to house extensive working-class populations.

In 1791, at the behest of George Washington, French-born engineer and architect Pierre L'Enfant devised a plan for the city of Washington consisting of an urban grid with intersecting diagonal avenues superimposed on it. These diagonals radiated from the two most significant points on the map—the sites set aside for edifices for Congress (the US Capitol) and

Montgomery Meigs, a career United States Army officer and civil engineer, painted this backyard scene at the rear of Franklin Row along K Street between Twelfth and Thirteenth Streets NW in 1850. It depicts vegetable gardens and accessory buildings at the interior of the city square, as early city planners had envisioned and before the rise of alley dwellings. (Library of Congress.)

the president. The grid streets ran north-south and east-west, dividing the city into four quadrants (NE, NW, SE, and SW) with the Capitol as the center point. Where the grid and the diagonals converged, large and smaller open spaces—today's public circles and squares, triangular parks, and small "pocket parks"—added scale and visual appeal to the vast city plan. The "squares" between the streets and avenues actually ranged in shape and size from large and small

rectangles or squares to irregular polygons or triangles. The first published plan of the city of Washington in 1792, as redrawn by surveyor and engineer Andrew Ellicott (who succeeded L'Enfant), did not yet detail the subdivision of the large city squares into either lots or interior alleys. Historians such as Daniel D. Swinney in his 1938 dissertation, "Washington: A City of Beauty and a City of Slums," surmised that L'Enfant purposely provided for abnormally large lots

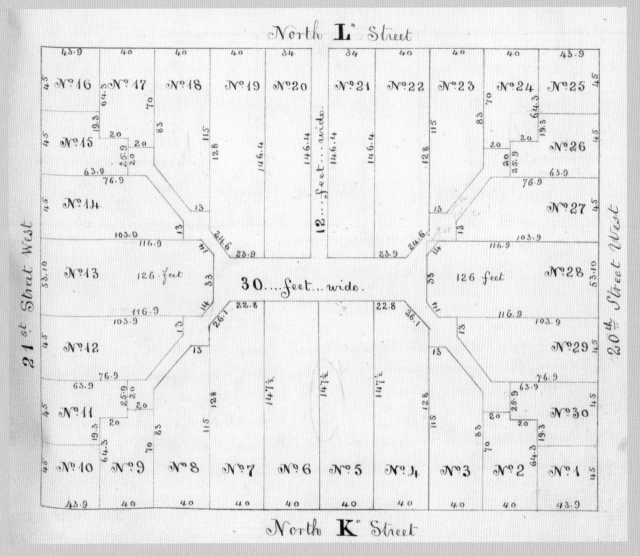

Alley configurations ranged from the most common *H*- and *I*-shaped forms to diagonal, straight, irregular, or *X*-shaped forms, as shown in this 1796 plat of square 76, between Twentieth, Twenty-First, K, and L Streets NW. (DC Office of the Surveyor Land Record Management System, Record of Squares.)

to encourage the development of detached homes and gardens for wholesome living in the city. The free-standing houses on gracious, landscaped lots provided safety from fire as well as enough land for kitchen gardens at the rear. The houses with their landscaped gardens would occupy the front of the lot, while vegetable gardens, animal yards, and accessory buildings, including housing for the enslaved, would be at the rear and away from public view.[5]

Over the next few years, as the site for the nation's capital was meticulously surveyed, platted, and made ready for the sale of lots and the construction of buildings, alleys were fully introduced into the plan. Each of the city's 1,143 squares, as recorded in the official "Record of Squares," was uniquely shaped and sized, and most were open at the center with public alleys.[6] Rather than cutting directly through the square from one street to the other, however, these alleys were laid out in several different configurations, influenced by the shape of the square itself. The most common followed *H*- and *I*-shaped plans at the center of the squares where they stretched thirty feet wide.[7] These alleys, reached from the street by narrower alleys, or passageways just ten to fifteen feet wide, were completely concealed from public view and the surrounding streets.

The Rise of Inhabited Alleys

In its first half-century of existence, the city of Washington developed slowly. The reasons for this are many, but a lack of adequate federal government funding for the construction of public buildings and city infrastructure, an inability to secure credit locally or abroad to fund development, and poor lot sales in the newly laid-out city together discouraged private investment and settlement. On top of that and for many decades, doubts lingered over whether the seat of the federal government would remain in Washington.[8] More than a half-century after its establishment, Washington was a small southern city with just over fifty thousand inhabitants, including Whites and free or enslaved Blacks. White and Black residents lived throughout the city, though they were largely segregated spatially. Whites tended to live in the urban core in residential pockets clustered around the White House and the Capitol, often with enslaved servants housed in a wing of the principal residence, while free Blacks were found farther out along the then edges of the city, in the port town of Georgetown, and in the low-lying areas of Foggy Bottom and Southwest.[9] With no public transportation system yet in place, development was limited to the "walking city"—the distance people could comfortably walk to get to and from the city center and the source of jobs. Given the limited population and ample opportunities for residential growth in its early decades, the city's alleys existed only on paper. The nature of alleys, however, would change dramatically in the second half of the nineteenth century. During and after the Civil War, as the city experienced a significant increase in population and housing began to reach capacity on the major streets in the center city, property owners, real estate developers, and incoming residents looked to the resubdivision of the city's large lots and to its extensive network of alleys to increase opportunities for housing.

In the early 1870s and continuing for decades, owners of the large city lots that regularly stretched fifty to one

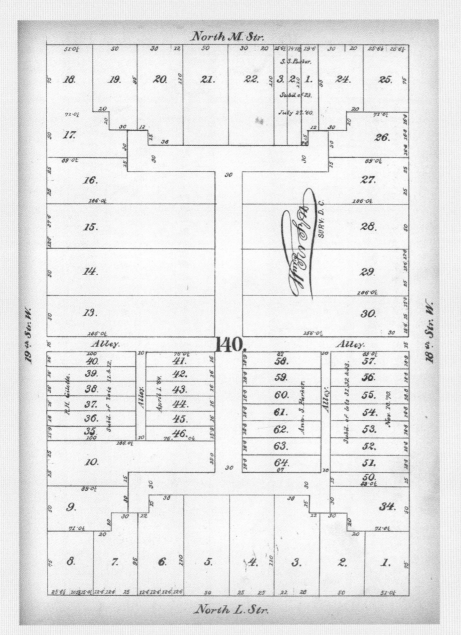

This 1873 plat of square 140 between Eighteenth, Nineteenth, L, and M Streets NW illustrates the changing character of city squares in the post–Civil War era as property owners divided the original large lots both in width to create narrower lots and lengthwise to create separate alley lots. These new alley lots (lots 41–46 and 58–64) were often separated from the street lots by narrower, ten-foot alleys laid between them. (E. F. M. Faehtz and F. W. Pratt, *Real Estate Directory of the City of Washington* [Washington, DC: Faehtz & Pratt, 1874], square book 4, folio 1150.)

hundred feet wide to accommodate detached dwellings began to divide their lots into narrower urban-sized ones measuring only twenty to twenty-five feet in width. These owners had recognized the opportunity for a new type of housing—the rowhouses that characterize DC's neighborhood streets today. These same property owners, many of whom were businessmen, entrepreneurs, builders, or real estate investors, also gained greater opportunities for housing (and a return on their investments) by cutting the deep lots off toward the rear. These subdivisions created smaller and entirely separate lots (called alley lots) that have alley-only frontages.[10] This phenomenon occurred for the most part after the Civil War as land values and rental costs were rising, making alley lots appealing both to those buying the lots and building the houses on them and to those residents who could not afford the rents of the rowhouses lining the city's major streets.

As these new lots were improved with dwellings and sold, the street-facing lots and alley lots were no longer owned by the same people, creating a unique relationship between the alley houses and the principal residences facing the public streets. In other southern cities with alley housing, such as Galveston, Texas, and Charleston, South Carolina, tenant houses or enslaved quarters that were sited along alleys shared the same lot as the main house, and although they were separated from the main house by a garden or court, they still faced the house and the public street.[11] In DC, alley dwellings were not oriented to the principal residence in front of it or to the street but instead opened directly onto the alleys within the interior of the square.

In addition to having their backs to the street-facing lots, alley dwellings were separated from them by fences, stables, and sheds, which the street-facing lot owners built to intentionally cut off their own views of the alleys.

During the second half of the nineteenth century, as more and more owners and builders divided their lots to create alley lots and built dwellings on them for rental income, the interior blocks of the pedestrian city came to house a sizable segment of the city's population. According to research by historian James Borchert in his seminal *Alley Life in Washington*, 11 percent of the population (18,978 persons) lived in the city's alleys by the end of the nineteenth century.[12]

Although this development pattern largely took root during and after the Civil War, some alleys were inhabited before the war. In 1858 there were at least forty-nine separate alleys housing 348 households.[13] The history of these pre–Civil War alley dwellings is unclear. While some published histories on Washington claim that the first alley dwellings were built as quarters for the enslaved, there is no solid evidence for that. Housing reformer Edith Elmer Wood in *The Housing of the Unskilled Wage Earner: America's Next Problem* posits that before emancipation, charitable organizations as well as individual property owners may have built temporary housing at the rear of their lots and along the alleys for those escaping slavery and in desperate need of shelter.[14]

On the other hand, Borchert believes that the first alley dwellings were more likely constructed to accommodate recent European immigrants and unskilled workers. As a case in point, he points to an account

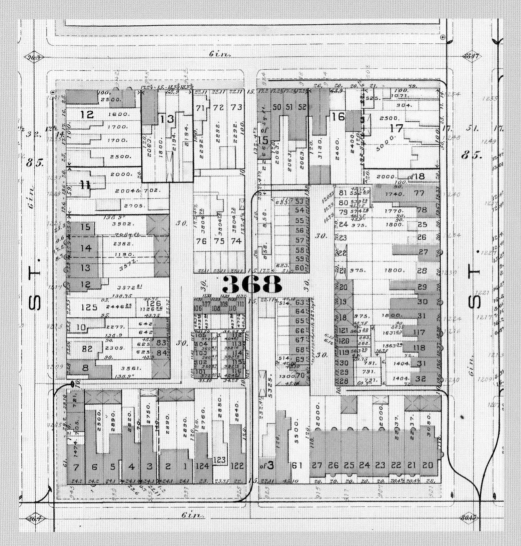

This detail from an 1892 map shows an almost fully built-up Blagden Alley in square 368 between Ninth, Tenth, M, and N Streets NW. The various stems of the *H*-shaped alley are filled with rows of modest brick and wooden alley dwellings, just twelve feet wide. Larger high-style Victorian dwellings lining the principal streets enclose the "hidden" alley. (G. M. Hopkins, *Surveys and Plats of Properties in the City of Washington, District of Columbia*, 1892, plate 28, Library of Congress, Geography and Map Division.)

Although located immediately behind street-facing houses, alley houses were visually isolated from them. Often fences, stables, and sheds at the rear of street lots, such as this rare surviving nineteenth-century row located at the rear of the 600 block of G Street SE, created further physical barriers between the street and alley houses and their residents. (Photo by Jamie Williams, 2021.)

recorded by Daniel Swinney for his 1938 dissertation on alley dwellings and housing reform. Swinney interviewed an elderly man and longtime resident of Foggy Bottom who recalled that a property owner in the neighborhood, C. H. Snow—co-owner of the *Daily National Intelligencer* newspaper—had built a greenhouse along with the four houses in the square's *I*-shaped alley before the Civil War. The elderly man recollected that Snow rented the houses to Irish immigrants, one of whom worked for him in his greenhouse.[15] Borchert contends that other inhabited alleys started in similar fashion, whereby one or more

property owner constructed small houses at the rear of their lots and rented them to free workers in need of affordable housing.

During the Civil War, particularly after slavery was abolished in the District of Columbia in 1862, and immediately after the war, an estimated forty thousand African Americans streamed into Washington. The city was totally unprepared for this increase in population. Adequate housing and places of shelter were not even available for persons with income, much less for those fleeing slavery or recently emancipated with no resources at all.[16] But wartime demand for labor

Wooden alley houses such as the ones shown in this photograph were built in the pre– and post–Civil War years to accommodate an influx of African Americans coming to the city to escape slavery or those recently emancipated. The number of inhabited alleys would grow from forty-nine in 1858 to over three hundred by the end of the nineteenth century. (DC History Center, James Borchert Alley Life Photograph Collection, BO-012.)

was high, so most of the incoming residents found work and built makeshift shelters wherever they could, many at the interior of the city's squares along the alleys. This development pattern greatly contributed to an increase in the number of inhabited alleys and to a discernible shift in their racial composition. Though later reports describe the "mean" cabins as having dirt floors, walls of boards with holes, and roofs of tin, tar, felt, and rags, newspaper and other accounts of the time reveal little specific information about the alleys or housing conditions. An 1865 story in the *Daily National Intelligencer* described the rise

of alley dwellings, noting "all sorts and sizes of them may be found, wedged in every conceivable shape into vacant spaces and yards and alleys."[17] One year later, the superintendent of police highlighted the rise of inhabited alleys, calling attention to the miserable conditions under which these newcomers were living, where "decent living is impossible."[18]

Georgetown, with its already sizable free Black population, became a haven for incoming African Americans. Men, women, and children escaping slavery in Virginia crossed the Potomac River to Georgetown where they settled in Herring Hill at

Civil War–era reports describe the makeshift alley housing built in Washington to shelter the thousands of Black fugitives or emancipated slaves fleeing from across the South as "mean" cabins. They had dirt floors, walls of boards with holes, and roofs of tin, tar, felt, and rags. Some Civil War–era alley dwellings still stood into the twentieth century, such as those shown in this 1903 photograph. (Committee on the Improvement of Housing Conditions, *From Associated Charities, Annual Report 1903–1904*, Catholic University of America Archives.)

Union and Liberty Streets

To assist the country's four million formerly enslaved after the Civil War, the federal government created the Freedmen's Bureau in 1865 and named as its director Gen. Oliver Otis Howard, a decorated Civil War veteran, White abolitionist, and one of the founders of Howard University. Howard led the Freedmen's Bureau in its purchase of a 375-acre tract of land in Southeast, where the agency planned a residential subdivision to house African American refugees who had come to the city during and after the Civil War. In addition to developing the freedmen's village (called Barry's Farm after James Barry, the pre–Civil War owner of the land, but officially named Potomac City and later Hillsdale), Howard appears also to have looked to the interiors of the city's squares to house the newly emancipated, many of whom he described as being "crowded together in miserable abodes" and in "wretched hovels not fit for human beings."[20] Under his presidency, Howard University purchased two large and undeveloped Capitol Hill squares (1054 and 1055 between Fourteenth, Fifteenth, and C Streets and Constitution Avenue NE) and in 1868 resubdivided them with two minor streets cutting through the squares. The new streets, named Union and Liberty, and the narrow fourteen-foot-wide lots lining them, provide a clue that Howard intended to accommodate housing for the formerly enslaved. Several pairs of modest dwellings (still standing in the 200 block of Fourteenth Street NE, square 1055) were built, but for unknown reasons a more comprehensive development like that of Barry's Farm never panned out. The two block-long minor streets through the squares were later renamed, and remain, Fourteenth Place NE.[21]

Georgetown's Black population grew during the Civil War. The alley dwellings pictured in this present-day photograph of Poplar Street NW (formerly Poplar Alley), which accommodated part of this influx, are the city's oldest surviving alley dwellings. (Photo by author, 2021.)

Georgetown's eastern edge, in areas south of M Street close to the port, and in the alleys, such as Poplar Alley and Bell's Court (today's Pomander Walk).[19] The incoming African American population, up from 1,935 persons before the Civil War to 3,271 in 1870, joined the other Black residents as laborers, cooks, drivers, washerwomen, dressmakers, and domestics. Despite the relative economic stability for Black Georgetowners, their housing options were limited.

Before the Civil War, 65 percent of the city's alley residents were White; in 1871, 81 percent of all alley residents were African American, more than double the prewar percentage.[22] The number, size, and segregated nature of the inhabited alleys continued to grow throughout the second half of the nineteenth century, and by 1897, 93 percent of all alley residents were African American.[23] Essentially secluded from the public, the city's poorest and mostly Black residents lived with their houses and lives facing inwardly to the alleys, while the wealthier and majority White residents occupied the adjacent and surrounding houses along the city's major streets and avenues.

Alley Names

When the plan for the city of Washington was published in 1792, its streets were named and numbered according to a system in which the US Capitol formed the central axis. From there, north-south streets followed a sequential numbering system, east-west streets were lettered in alphabetical order, and avenues (always diagonal) were named for the existing states. The alleys were left unnamed and were referred to simply as the alley between the public streets that bound its square. Many of the alleys were later named by the real estate investor or builder who erected the alley dwellings, like Groff Court on Capitol Hill, Snows Court in Foggy Bottom, Keady's (Cady's) Alley in Georgetown, and Blagden's Alley in Shaw. In other cases, residents living in or outside the alleys or census takers and city directory canvassers named the alleys in often pointedly descriptive ways that stuck. Some described the alleys' physical layout, like Zig Zag Alley in Southwest, or its proximity to adjacent places, like Navy Place Alley in Southeast (near the Navy Yard) and St. Matthew's Court NW (behind St. Matthew's Cathedral). Others pointed to the demographics of the original alley inhabitants, like Limerick Court in Southwest (between Second, Third, and D Streets and Virginia Avenue). Others referred to industrial or other uses found in the alleys, like Ice Alley in Northwest, home to an ice manufacturing plant; Hook and Ladder Alley off Massachusetts Avenue NW, which housed a volunteer fire department; and Moonshine Alley, presumably the site of a still. Other names conjured up more bucolic environs, like Peach Alley, Pear Tree Alley, Acorn Alley, and even Willow Tree Alley, which ironically by the late nineteenth century was considered one of the most crime-ridden alleys in the city. Other alleys had more sinister names, like Knife Alley, Fighting Alley, and Blood Alley.

One such alley on Capitol Hill, known in the 1880s for rowdy activity and altercations that required regular police intervention, earned its name, Tiger Alley. The local press reported, "The attention of the authorities will be called to the noisy and turbulent character of parties who are allowed to occupy the premises where shrieks of women, coupled with oaths from men, are frequently heard. Wednesday night last, at about 10 o'clock, for squares around, cries of murder were heard emanating from the houses, which attracted a crowd of persons to the scene."[24] For years neighbors in the streets surrounding Tiger Alley sought to have the three wooden dwellings within the alley torn down. In 1892 Charles Gessford, a local builder who was a prolific builder of rowhouses on Capitol Hill, replaced the wooden structures with a neat row of ten two-story brick dwellings and renamed the alley Gessford Court. While the name Tiger Alley has long been forgotten, Gessford Court and its dwellings survive as a quiet urban oasis that is today home to urban professionals.

Alley Dwellings

The first-generation alley dwellings were mostly wooden buildings, one and two stories tall, built individually, in pairs, and in small rows. The houses, with walls and roofs clad with wood boards and scavenged materials, sat directly on the ground with floors of tamped dirt. They had no plumbing, heat, or insulation systems and were often sited adjacent to horse stables, coal yards, or refuse heaps. Residents relied on communal water pumps and outhouses.

The poor drainage systems, absence of sewers, common water sources, and the dwellings' proximity to stables all contributed to unhealthy and insanitary living conditions that attracted the attention of early humanitarians. In response to their lobbying, Congress established the city's first Board of Health in 1871, tasked in part with studying housing conditions in the city and condemning dwellings that were deemed unfit for human habitation. In its study, the board reported that many alleys were "lined on both sides with miserable dilapidated shanties, patched and filthy," with no pure water supply, no drainage, no fire protections, leaking privies, and in "bad sanitary condition generally."[25] During its first years in operation, the board identified 958 houses in the city as "unfit for human habitation," oversaw the demolition of about 300 of these dwellings, and recommended hundreds more for rehabilitation. Within a few years of its creation, however, the Board of Health was reorganized and the condemnation proceedings of insanitary buildings were halted. This change came about as the owners and builders who were benefiting financially

The row of one-story alley dwellings shown here on Trumbull Court NW was built in the years just after the Civil War. The now-demolished houses stood across the street from the still-standing Bryant Street Pumping Station in the 300 block of Bryant Street NW. (DC History Center, John P. Wymer Collection, WY 1080.)

from the construction of alley dwellings used their political influence to undermine the early humanitarians and upend the government's effort to identify and eliminate insanitary housing in the city.[26]

After the Civil War, the federal government under President Ulysses S. Grant sought to assure the country that Washington would not only remain a permanent seat of the federal government but also a fitting symbol of unity. An expanding federal bureaucracy and heavy investment in vast citywide infrastructure

This photograph of an unnamed alley illustrates the nature of buildings in the alleys during the post–Civil War years. During the 1870s insanitary conditions in the city's inhabited alleys attracted the attention of early humanitarians. (Library of Congress.)

improvements spurred widespread development and confidence in the capital city, encouraging a dramatic increase in population. As a need for housing ensued (for both existing residents who lacked adequate housing and incoming workers), owners, real estate speculators, and builders continued to subdivide their long lots into alley lots, and alley dwelling construction boomed.[27] From 1877 to 1892 approximately twenty-five hundred alley dwellings were approved for construction as part of the city's building permit process, and probably many more were actually erected.[28] While many of these alley dwellings were constructed by people involved in the real estate industry, many others were built by or purchased after construction by individuals for the rental income. In

the early 1910s housing reformer Edith Elmer Wood identified forty-seven different owners of alley dwellings in just four of the city's alleys, including lawyers, clerks, shop owners, a dentist, a mapmaker, an architect, a seamstress, and a dealer in tombstones.[29] These investors were largely absentee owners. They held on to their properties for years and even decades, collecting monthly rent payments yet rarely, if ever, engaged with the renters, inspected the houses, or provided needed repairs or services for the aging and heavily used structures.[30]

At the start of this alley dwelling building boom, the Board of Public Works (established during the city's short-lived territorial government of 1871–74) adopted the first comprehensive set of building regulations

In 1872 the city implemented its first set of building codes that forbade the construction of wooden buildings. In the 1880s and early 1890s thousands of new alley dwellings were erected of brick rather than wood. (Library of Congress.)

Although modest in size and lacking in amenities, alley dwellings often featured some degree of ornamentation. Prolific Capitol Hill builder Charles Gessford constructed a group of ten dwellings with corbeled brick cornices and projecting hood molds over their windows and doors in the alley bounded by Eleventh, Twelfth, and C Streets and Independence Avenue SE. The alley, named in 1904 for Gessford, retains all ten of those dwellings built by him. (Photo by author, 2021.)

in the District of Columbia. These would not only impact the nature of building along the city's major streets but also in its alleys.[31] Like those adopted by other cities in the aftermath of the Great Chicago Fire of 1871, the regulations showed a concern for the safety and sanitation of city residents. For instance, to deter fires, the regulations forbade the construction of wooden buildings in the "densely populated sections" of the city. Revised regulations in 1877, aimed at improving the sanitation of housing, required that any newly constructed buildings had to be equipped with either a toilet (called a "water closet") or an outhouse. In 1887 regulations forbade the construction of dwellings less than twelve feet in width or fronting on any open space less than twenty feet in width.

During the 1880s and early 1890s, alley dwellings followed a standard building form: they were two-story brick structures (no longer wooden) and most often arranged in pairs or in longer rows of four or more. They were set on low foundations rather than directly on the ground, covered with sloped roofs, sheathed in tin, and shared a common cornice line. The front facades spanned only the required twelve-to-fifteen-foot width as the changing code demanded, allowing for a narrow door and window on the first story and two windows above. Though modest in size and architectural exuberance compared to their street-facing counterparts, these alley dwellings were solidly built. Victorian-era detailing such as corbeled brick cornices, window hoods, and other decorative treatments often embellished the modest dwellings.

The houses extended twenty feet deep, with ten-foot-deep single-story lean-to sheds at the rear housing the

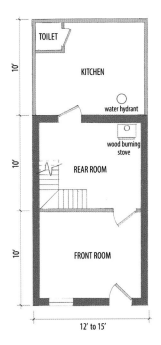

The ground-level layout of a typical two-story alley dwelling. (Kim Elliott.)

kitchen, a toilet, and a water hydrant, the only source of water. Beyond the sheds, alley dwellings generally had tiny rear yards. Inside, alley houses typically consisted of four small rooms. The first floor housed a front and rear room, both approximately twelve by ten feet, for living, sleeping, and dining. The second floor held two bedrooms.

City building codes dramatically improved the quality of construction of alley dwellings, but the houses still lacked basic amenities such as indoor plumbing. Furthermore, once they had built and rented the dwellings, property owners did little to maintain them. Health codes were not regularly enforced, and when they were, owners often chose to

Kitchens, like the one shown in this 1935 photograph by Farm Security Administration (FSA) photographer Carl Mydans, were located in tiny, one-story lean-tos at the rear of the alley dwellings. (Library of Congress.)

Alley Population

The population curve in the city's alleys, based on city directory listings, police reports, and alley inventories, began with a steep ascent followed by a slow decline. In 1858, when the city's total population was about fifty thousand, there were 49 inhabited alleys housing 348 persons. By 1871 there were 118 alleys, home to 1,500 inhabitants. By 1897 there were 303 inhabited alleys housing 18,978 residents—figures that remained relatively unchanged for the next decade while the city's total population rose steadily from about 278,000 in 1900 to 331,000 in 1910. After 1912 the population of the city's alleys began a slow but progressive decline. In 1912 an inventory of the city's alleys recorded 275 inhabited alleys with 3,337 dwellings housing 16,000 persons; by 1932 those numbers were down to 188 inhabited alleys with 1,947 alley dwellings housing 5,988 residents.[33] By 1970 the city directories listed 20 inhabited alleys with 192 heads of households.[34]

A study of historic alley buildings by the DC Historic Preservation Office in 2011–13 identified approximately twenty alleys within the confines of the original city, comprising just over one hundred surviving nineteenth-century alley dwellings. These dwellings—not necessarily still inhabited and certainly not by the urban poor—represent a small fraction of the historic numbers of dwellings. Still, notable clusters of alley dwellings remain on Capitol Hill, in Georgetown, in Foggy Bottom, and downtown in Blagden Alley and Naylor Court. Today new alley housing is joining this historic building stock as former stables and garages are renovated and converted to residential use, new alley dwellings are constructed on vacant alley lots, and accessory dwelling units rise at the rear of street-facing lots.

pay fines over making repairs. Humanitarians, social reformers, and others concerned with housing the poor pressed the city's congressional overseers for action. This outcry led Congress to pass a law in 1892 that banned the construction of dwellings in alleys less than thirty feet wide and not supplied with sewerage and water mains. While this law halted the construction of new buildings, it did not require the retrofitting of existing alleys or the removal of existing alley dwellings. In 1897, seven years after this prohibition, 18,978 people lived in 303 inhabited alleys in the city.[32] Although these numbers represent a historical peak and the number of inhabited alleys and alley dwellings declined over time, life in the city's alleys would continue for decades to come.

CHAPTER 2   Alley Life

LIFE IN WASHINGTON's inhabited alleys was un-equivocally challenging in the late nineteenth and early twentieth centuries. Bustling with people, animals, and industry, the alleys, with tight rows of tiny dwellings and adjacent stables and industry, were undesirable and unhealthy places to live. Humanitarians, housing reformers, and politicians universally condemned them as "slums" and places of "evil" or, in President Theodore Roosevelt's words, "breeding grounds of vice and decay."[1] Until the mid-twentieth century, only the city's poorest residents who had no housing alternatives lived in the alleys.

Yet for these "alleyites,"[2] as contemporary newspapers termed them, the alleys were home. Despite their squalid and neglected conditions, the alleys were a place of family and community, a place of work and livelihood, and a place of safety from the inhospitable outside world. Alley residents generally lived, socialized, worked, played, and banded together to help each other through the daily hardships of life and death.

Historically, information about alley life has been filtered through the prism of humanitarians, housing reformers, muckraking journalists, and politicians intent on eradicating alleys and their dwellings. African Americans and Whites equally condemned alley conditions and their deleterious effects on people. In 1901 Black sociologist, historian, and civil rights activist W. E. B. Du Bois proclaimed inhabited alleys to be "deadly to civilization," just as the newspaper *Colored American* opined, "Alley life in Washington, as in other cities, contributes more to crime and suffering than any other source of evil."[3]

Sociologists and humanitarians who conducted studies of the city's inhabited alleys and whose stated intention was to improve the lives of the poor painted a singularly bleak picture of alley life, with its physically unhealthy conditions and morally depraved inhabitants. Health and police department reports recorded high rates of disease, death, and crime. Largely to illustrate and argue their points, the humanitarians provided excruciatingly detailed reports on the squalor and overcrowded conditions and high levels of unemployment, disease, and criminal activity. These accounts often included photographs of the most extreme and negative conditions.

In 1909 sociologist and photographer Lewis Hine captured this photograph of Purdy's Court, an alley just northwest of the Capitol and now subsumed into the US Capitol grounds. Working for the National Child Labor Committee, Hine used photography to expose the harsh working conditions of children but also, as in this case, to showcase the insanitary living conditions of the urban and rural poor. (George Eastman Museum, Rochester, NY, Lewis Wickes Hine Collection.)

As a photographer for the FSA seeking to document rural and urban life in America, Edwin Rosskam took many photos in Washington's alleys. His 1941 photograph of children gathered at the center of an unnamed DC alley helping to unload crates and boxes to be used for cooking and heating illustrates a strong sense of community in the alleys. (Library of Congress.)

FSA photographer Carl Mydans spent much of 1935 photographing the alleys of Washington, DC. His photograph of this outhouse immediately adjacent to a water pump was intended to illustrate the insanitary and unhealthy living conditions that prevailed in the city's alleys. (Library of Congress.)

In this 1935 photograph, Mydans captured the interior of a typical alley kitchen, located in a small wing at the back of the dwelling. (Library of Congress.)

Through these illustrated documents, reformers aimed to convince politicians and the public at large that the only solution to ridding the city of its slums was to eradicate its inhabited alleys and alley dwellings. In proposing alley eradication, reformers rarely considered the effect of displacement on those who had no alternative housing. Some Black leaders, such as Dr. Rev. John Milton Waldron, president of the Alley Improvement Association, believed that instead of eliminating the alleys, which offered home and community to the city's poorest residents, more attention should be placed on making them sanitary. He and his nonprofit organization, founded in 1908, argued that the city should improve the alleys and the lives of their inhabitants so that alleys "cease to be plague spots."[4]

Like Waldron, others documenting the city's alleys were more hopeful about life there. Daniel D. Swinney, who wrote his dissertation on alley dwellings and alley housing in DC in 1938, interviewed alley residents and observed that they were bound together and most had no desire to leave. One elderly gentleman proclaimed, "Of course I live here because of cheap rent but if I had lots of money I wouldn't want to move.... Most of us are poor and live in bad houses but we have a good time."[5] Godfrey Frankel, who photographed the alleys of Southwest in 1943, later recalled, "I was amazed when I first saw these alley houses—monotonous, drab, two-story brick dwellings stretching a block long, and people spilling out of the doorways directly onto the street." He soon discovered a "specialness" to the alleys, however, and saw them as thriving neighborhoods: "Even though my initial motive was to reveal inadequate housing, poverty and squalor, there was something else I was seeing, too. . . . I attempted to capture it."[6]

In the 1970s and early 1980s, historian James Borchert conducted extensive research and analysis of alley life by examining the reports and photographs of the housing reformers and humanitarians along with other historical records. Borchert's research, like Frankel's personal discoveries decades earlier, led him to conclude that in spite of the abject poverty, overcrowding, isolation from the outside, and unhealthy conditions, DC's inhabited alleys were tight-knit and supportive communities that teemed with life. In his book *Alley Life in Washington* and other publications, Borchert convincingly illustrates that alley residents, faced with their exceedingly harsh and challenging lives and environments, transformed their spaces and built deeply rooted social and community networks.

A scene captured in Dixon Court (between Third, 4 1/2, H, and I Streets SW) by Godfrey Frankel. In 1995 the Smithsonian Institution Press published Godfrey's photographs in *In the Alleys: Kids in the Shadow of the Capital*. (www.facebook.com/godfreyfrankel.)

This 1923 scene of residents walking together to and from their homes in Blagden Alley provides a good illustration of the tight-knit nature of alley communities, despite the hardships of alley living. (Library of Congress.)

Children playing in an alley in 1923. (DC Public Library, People's Archive, Historic Images Collection, 139.)

This photograph in Cecil Alley NW titled *Boy Gang* appeared in the 1903 annual report of the Associated Charities of Washington, D.C. In the first decades of the twentieth century, Cecil Alley in Georgetown was home to working-class White residents, while the adjacent Cherry Hill Alley was entirely Black-occupied. (Catholic University of America Archives, Associated Charities, Annual Report 1903–1904, Committee on the Improvement of Housing Conditions.)

Physical Environment and Community

Because the alleys occupied the interior of the city's squares and were concealed from public view, alley residents were physically and visually segregated from their street neighbors and outsiders. In part due to this physical isolation, property owners and the city regularly neglected their duties to service, clean, and maintain the alleys and their dwellings, the owners escaping housing code violations and other penalties in the process. As a result, alley dwellings fell into poor physical condition. Outhouses were often overflowing, piles of trash could be found in heaps in alley spaces, and rodents ran rampant through the alleys and the houses.

Housing reformers largely blamed the insanitary conditions on the hidden and substandard nature of the alley environment. Borchert, on the other hand, acknowledged the sanitation issues but found that the physical confines of the alley rather encouraged the positive development of intimate, caring, and self-help communities where everyone knew one another. Off the regular vehicular routes, alleys offered open space and opportunities for informal gathering, socializing, relaxing, and playing. The alleys provided, in essence, a shared front yard and nurturing community to those living in tiny alley dwellings abutting and facing each other across the narrow thirty-foot ways.[7] Many historical photographs, like those taken by photographers with the Farm Security Administration and meant to illustrate the poor housing conditions in the city's alleys, capture instead a palpable sense of community. Photos of children playing, people socializing, and families posing outside their dwellings imbue that "specialness" of place that Frankel felt as he wandered the alleys of Southwest with camera in hand.

Family Structure and Employment

According to many of the reports and studies on the city's alley housing, alleys provided both transient and long-term living quarters for the inhabitants. Many of those who immigrated to the city and began their lives in the alleys were able to find good-paying and reliable jobs that enabled them to move out of the alleys into street-facing houses. Others could either not afford to leave or chose to remain, and many lived in the alleys for decades, close to families, friends, schools, and churches. Despite cheek-by-jowl accommodations in small rows of narrow dwellings, the alleys offered a degree of autonomy. As one alley dweller noted in 1915, "better [to] have a little place than have a big place and fill it full of roomers."[8] During the 1930s when the city began building public housing in the less populated areas of Northeast and Southeast, many alley residents did not want to move. They had deep roots in their communities, and despite the lure of sanitary living conditions such as running water, inside toilets, and electricity, they were reluctant to relocate far from their schools, churches, friends, and family.

Alley dwellings, which rented on average for about nine dollars per month in the early twentieth century, housed the city's lowest-income residents. Yet, given the scarcity of housing in the city then, especially for the poorest residents, property owners made substantial profits on the rental of alley dwellings during an era when their right to do so was unquestioned. In her 1896 report to the Women's Anthropological Society, sociologist Mary Clare de Graffenried noted, "One conclusion at least is evident: that rents in these alleys are dear, considering the accommodations and environment."[9] In her 1913 study of eighty-eight dwellings in four DC alleys, housing reformer Edith Elmer Wood found that the average return on investment was 16 percent, about twice what was considered a fair return on street property.[10] In one notable exception, Wood discovered that while the owner of the alley dwelling was charging rents that provided him what was considered a fair return of 12.5 percent, the person he was renting to was then subletting the rooms for more than double what it cost him. In this case, the middleman was a White immigrant grocer who ran the store on the ground floor of a Madison Alley dwelling (the site of the DC Convention Center today).[11] Rather than living above the store, which was typical for the era, the grocer rented the upstairs rooms out on a weekly basis, with one family per room, some with five or six members to a family, garnering himself a comfortable rental income. In 1948 Mrs. Emma Cobb who lived at 26 Dingman Place, with its four small rooms, paid twenty-eight dollars per month in rent to her landlord. This landlord was a tenant himself and rented the property from the owner for half that price. The owner, who lived in Chevy Chase, Maryland, had purportedly not visited her investment property in years.[12]

On average, rents were lower in the alleys than on the street, but they were still high compared to earnings, making it difficult for alley dwellers to save enough money to transition out of the alleys and into street-facing houses. "We [could] have bought this house . . . [many times] over, been here so long paying rent," noted one alley resident.[13]

Many alley dwellers, unable to afford the rents, even sublet rooms themselves. This in turn led to overcrowding and to a wide array of family structures. Multigenerational households with extended family members, households with boarders, single mothers with children with different paternities, and more traditional nuclear families all shared space in tight alley quarters. Reformers decried these overcrowded and unorthodox households, claiming that such situations, especially where single men were involved, invited immoral behavior and activity. Conversely, Borchert found that the tight and crowded quarters encouraged more healthful outdoor living and a communal social order. Historical images of alley dwellings with their windows and doors open and furniture in the alleys confirm this perspective. Life spilled out of the tiny houses and into the public realm, not only expanding the living quarters of the individual houses but also promoting social interaction between residents. In addition, and even acknowledged by humanitarians, extended family members and boarders not only contributed to the cost of rent but they also helped care for the children and with household chores.

Almost everyone who lived in the alleys, including children, worked to support the household. The vast majority of male "heads of household" were unskilled, semiskilled, or menial service workers. Those who worked skilled and semiskilled jobs were listed in census records as barbers, carpenters, blacksmiths,

An alley family poses for FSA photographer Edwin Rosskam outside their dwelling in 1941. Devoid of traffic, alleys provided communal living space for residents and an escape from the tight interiors of the dwellings. As alley historian James Borchert noted, "it was difficult to know where the alley house ended and the alley commons began." (Library of Congress.)

A multigenerational alley family poses for a photograph taken by FSA photograph Edwin Rosskam in 1941. According to Rosskam's caption, the older woman worked as a cleaning woman for the federal government. (Library of Congress.)

plasterers, brick masons, and the like, but the vast majority were noted simply as laborers, hod carriers, handymen, and "rag men" or "junk dealers."[14] In a study of a single alley (identified as "Alley K") conducted in 1915 by the Associated Charities of Washington, D.C., the chronicler, Mary Cromwell, noted that many of the male alley dwellers were street cleaners earning "a dollar and a half per day."[15]

Most of these jobs were seasonal and irregular, leaving many alley residents unemployed for days or weeks at a time. Reformers who witnessed men in the alleys during work hours characterized them as "idle," even though they recognized that their situation was largely a result of job discrimination. In her report, Cromwell wrote, "The men . . . are industrious, but as the restrictions of labor, on account of color, limit them to few openings, quite often a number are apparently idle and without work."[16] Those jobs that were open to them—unskilled jobs in construction—were also weather-dependent. The women of the alleys, according to Cromwell, referred to the male residents as "sunshine" men since the only jobs they could get—unskilled labor jobs in building construction—depended on good weather.[17]

Women alley residents often had more regular employment than the men. "The women, without exception, do laundry work. . . . Continually complaining but without redress, they accept the inadequate wages for their services," reported Cromwell.[18] As alley dwellings lacked indoor plumbing, the residents often did their laundry together in the public space by the water hydrant. They would then hang it to dry in their small rear yards where clotheslines were stretched from poles erected on the roofs of their rear sheds and

Many historical photographs, like this one taken by FSA photographer Carl Mydans in 1935, show laundry hanging in the small backyards or across the narrow alleys. (Library of Congress.)

Newsboys on the grounds of the US Capitol in 1912, photographed by Lewis Hines. This group, ranging in age from eight to twelve, lived in nearby Schott's Alley (present site of the Hart and Dirksen Senate Office Buildings). (Library of Congress.)

reached by ladder stairs in the yards. One elderly alley resident, who supported her extended family of six by taking in laundry, injured herself and had to spend a month in the hospital after falling from a broken ladder stair while hanging the laundry. Although the landlord was aware of the condition of the ladder stair, he had refused to fix it.[19]

Alley children also worked. The boys did "junk" work, collecting items from trash heaps that could be reused or sold, and ran errands. Girls washed dishes and undertook other household chores. Many alley children held actual jobs to help support the family and pay for their own clothes. A 1912 survey of child labor in Washington by Lewis Hine, a photographer for the National Child Labor Committee, revealed that young alley children were employed as newsboys, working long hours into the night selling papers, while others worked at Washington's markets.[20]

Schott's Alley NE, with the Russell Senate Office Building in the background, shot in 1941 by FSA photographer Marion Post Wolcott. Schott's Alley was home to both Black and White residents. (Library of Congress.)

Historically, many alleys, as reported in the press and by housing reformers, were notoriously dangerous places. Period newspapers, with their predilection toward the shocking, recorded innumerable accounts of criminal activity within the city's inhabited alleys, from gambling to knife fights and worse. But those who lived there had a different perspective. In 1994 Lawrence E. Boone, who grew up in Dixon Court in Southwest before its 1954 demolition, recollected, "A lot of people used to say that Dixon Court was bad, but the people in Dixon Court didn't think so. The reputation was bad. I was a little ashamed at being from Dixon Court. I didn't want anyone to know. But I loved being from Dixon Court. I loved coming back there."[21]

Progressive Era reports universally describe the fear and intimidation that outsiders felt upon entering the alleys and the protections that police and others took upon entering. But if you were a resident of the alley, it was a safe space, recalled former alley resident Roberta Patrick in 1994. "If you lived in an alley, you were called 'alley rat' on top of everything else. It left you feeling bad. The only protection you had was to get back home to the alleys, where you were safe."[22]

Borchert argues that alley residents felt threatened by intruders and thus developed techniques to protect each other and maintain control over their "turf." Due to the narrow points of entry into the alleys and the tight clustering of buildings, residents were aware of outsiders entering their domain. For their own protection, residents confronted them, demanded to know the reason for their presence, and regularly intimidated them, including through verbal and physical assault. The *Evening Star* reported on one such assault when two policemen attempted to arrest a "notorious colored woman . . . for being disorderly and blowing a tin horn." According to the account, "a large crowd of colored men and women attacked the officers with sticks and stones" before fellow officers came to their aid.[23] Such attacks played on the dangers and fear of alleys.

Those fears, combined with insanitary conditions of the city's inhabited alleys and the image that they presented in the nation's capital, contributed to persistent and organized efforts to eliminate them. As chapter 3 will illustrate, these social reform efforts were not immediate or even that effective. But between them and other transportation, social, and economic forces that occurred over the course of several decades, the number of residents living in the city's alleys would eventually begin to decline.

CHAPTER 3 Humanitarian Reform Efforts

FOR DECADES, beginning in the early 1870s as the construction of alley dwellings proliferated, social and humanitarian reformers concerned with housing the city's poor sounded a collective alarm over the appalling conditions of Washington's inhabited alleys and the threat they posed to public health. Nationwide, reformers were publishing exposés of the crowded and inhumane living conditions of the poorest residents in all American cities but especially the multistory tenements of New York City and Chicago, where renters crowded into tiny flats with bathrooms shared with multiple units. Individuals, charitable organizations, and other entities undertook studies, published reports, and took photographs of the housing conditions to raise social and political consciousness. Although well intentioned, these Progressive Era reformers who believed that cleaner cities made for better citizens also imposed their own paternalistic attitudes about what constituted appropriate behavior and activities, especially when it came to family structure, "illegitimate" children, "idleness," and other perceived moral shortcomings.

Dutch-born journalist Jacob Riis led the way in New York City and would soon make his way to

DC. In the 1880s Riis worked as a young police reporter for the *New York Tribune*, where he covered the most crime-ridden and poorest neighborhoods of the Lower East Side of Manhattan. Outraged by the overcrowded, unhygienic, and disease-ridden living conditions of the immigrant community, Riis set about to make a difference. He wrote scathing articles detailing the horrific conditions of tenement housing and illustrated them with photographs to shock his readers. Through his muckraking journalism, he blamed the landlords, police, and corrupt politicians who exploited tenement residents for financial or political gain. As Riis explained, landlords commanded excessive rents for small, ill-maintained apartments and neglected basic upkeep and maintenance because they knew that the renters had no alternatives. Landlords paid off corrupt politicians and police who then deliberately ignored housing code violations.[1] Riis began giving lectures on his findings, and in 1890 he published his first book, *How the Other Half Lives*. Riis's revelations greatly influenced social reform efforts nationwide and contributed to passage of the New York State Tenement House Act of 1901. This law, which helped protect the housing rights of the poor, was the nation's strongest and served as a model for other states. It required high minimum standards for construction and sanitation in new housing, such as outward-facing windows in every room, an open courtyard, proper ventilation systems, indoor toilets, and fire safeguards.

"Unfit for Human Habitation"

Riis's New York City revelations influenced reformers in other cities to look more intensely at their own housing conditions.[2] In Washington the city's inhabited alleys shared many of the same pathologies as the multistoried, back-to-back tenements of the Lower East Side. Primitive alley houses, clustered along the city's alleys with minimal if any sanitary services, were often overcrowded as extended families and boarders shared the small quarters to make ends meet.

As alley dwellings emerged in a makeshift manner during and after the Civil War, DC officials and humanitarians became concerned about their conditions. In 1872 the city's Board of Health began a short-lived process of condemning alley houses deemed "unfit for human habitation." Two decades later, in 1892, Congress passed legislation that banned the construction of dwellings in alleys that were less than thirty feet wide. This legislation helped to stem the proliferation of new substandard spaces, but it did little to improve the existing conditions for the thousands of DC residents already living in alleys without basic amenities.[3] Some alleys held as many as fifty dwellings sheltering several hundred people. In 1897 Navy Place Alley in Southeast and Willow Tree Alley in Southwest, two

of the most populous of the city's inhabited alleys, recorded 344 and 328 inhabitants each.[4]

By the late nineteenth century, as housing conditions in DC worsened and as Riis's efforts in New York were proving effective, several charitable entities formed to help improve local housing conditions. In 1896 the Civic Center—a nonprofit established two years earlier specifically to improve DC housing conditions—collaborated with the Women's Anthropological Society of America (established in 1885) on a study of the city's inhabited alleys.[5] Volunteers conducted a month-long, house-by-house investigation of 191 dwellings in thirty-five alleys across the city. The data recorded alley width and configuration, housing construction materials, and access to running water, privies, and other services. The survey also recorded the proximity of alley dwellings to stables, their manure pits, and other unhealthy conditions. After collecting the information in the field, the Civic Center and the Women's Anthropological Society engaged labor researcher and writer Mary Clare de Graffenried to compile and analyze the findings. "Typical Alley Houses in Washington, D.C.," published by the Women's Anthropological Society in 1897, reported that the surveyors had recorded a variety of living conditions and recognized that some alleys and alley houses were well kept and sanitary but that, on average, the city's inhabited alleys were woefully overcrowded, insanitary, and unhealthy places that contributed to disease, criminal behavior, and vice.[6]

De Graffenried noted in her report that in more than half of the cases, alley dwellings were in "various states of decrepitude and decay." They were,

Navy Place Alley SE (between Sixth, Seventh, G, and I Streets SE) was regularly referred to as one of the city's most notorious alleys for its overpopulation, insanitary conditions, and criminal activity. In 1897 a police census recorded 344 residents there. This 1939 photograph was taken as the Alley Dwelling Authority was clearing the residents out of the alley in preparation for its demolition. (DC Housing Authority.)

Willow Tree Alley SW (located on the present-day site of the Wilbur Cohen Social Security Administration Building, on the south side of Independence Avenue SW), shown in this circa 1915 photograph, was consistently identified by housing reformers and journalists as one of the city's most overpopulated and crime-ridden alleys. An early twentieth-century account of the alley describes the "narrow and circuitous winding passages" leading to the interior court, shown here. (Photograph by Roy E. Haynes, Franklin D. Roosevelt Presidential Library, John Ihlder Collection.)

furthermore, "hidden away" and "difficult, even dangerous to access, off the policemen's beat, inviting lawlessness and crime."

De Graffenried's report described overflowing privies and houses located adjacent to stables, animals, manure pits, and other refuse piles, all of which gave off "dreadful stenches" and charged that the houses, without cellar or attic and with poor drainage, "inevitably cause disease." Period health reports show that alley residents carried a disproportionate burden of unhealthy conditions and disease. In 1910 the overall death rate was 17.56 persons per thousand for street dwellers and almost twice that at 30.09 persons per thousand for alley residents.[7]

The publication of "Typical Alley Houses in Washington, D.C." garnered the attention of housing reformers outside of Washington. One person in particular—Charles Weller, a social worker deeply concerned about housing the poor—would soon devote himself to the cause of improving housing and living conditions in the District, especially its alleys. Weller had worked at the Associated Charities of Chicago for eight years, and in 1900 he came to DC to take on the role as general secretary of the Associated Charities there. Established in 1881 and incorporated in 1882, the Associated Charities of Washington, D.C., was a private nonprofit whose mission was to bring about self-support, independence, and moral regeneration of the poor. While general secretary of DC's Associated Charities, Weller established the Committee on Friendly Visiting and the Committee on Improvement of Housing Conditions. Agents working for these committees visited hundreds of tenements, shanties, and alley dwellings throughout Washington in the early 1900s, collecting information about the lives and livelihoods of the residents and compiling their findings in a pamphlet that Weller then distributed to all members of Congress.[8] To better understand the lives of the poor and their living conditions, Weller also took up residency himself for various periods in one of the alleys and in several of the neighborhoods.[9]

Based on his own observations, along with the findings of the Committee on Improvement of Housing and the information already compiled by de Graffenried, Weller began a relentless campaign to educate the public, politicians, and the press on the horrific housing conditions in Washington. Weller gave lectures and testified in Congress and then began writing what would be the seminal book *Neglected Neighbors: Stories of Life in the Alleys, Tenements and Shanties of the National Capital*. The book, which was intended to advance his campaign for better housing, included extensive data, anecdotal case studies, and photographs that documented in graphic detail the most horrific and shocking living conditions of selected alleys. To capture the readers' attention, rather than provide statistics like many housing reports of the period were prone to do, Weller instead recounted stories about specific families. For instance, in describing overcrowded housing conditions in one alley, Weller did not simply note that a family of four sublet the kitchen lean-to of the dwelling in which several other families also lived—he described how "they dragged out greasy mattresses at night on which to sleep upon the floor." Weller's prose style, like that of other White Progressive Era chroniclers, is filled with cultural assumptions and racial prejudice. But even within that context, Weller largely condemned society for the housing ills of the poor and lobbied hard for governmental and civic involvement to improve them.[10]

During the first decade of the twentieth century when Weller and other social reformers were reporting on the unhealthy living conditions in the city's alleys, city leaders and politicians were in the throes of planning for the centennial celebration of the arrival of the federal government in Washington. The 1901 McMillan Plan, inspired by the City Beautiful movement—an urban planning reform philosophy that sought to introduce beauty and grandeur into cities to inspire civic virtue—proposed a comprehensive rebuilding of the city's monumental core. For Weller, these proposed plans of grand and classically inspired government buildings stood in stark contrast to the conditions in the city's alleys. He and others seized the opportunity to gain political momentum by publicizing the physical dichotomy between the city's existing federal buildings, with their gleaming white marble facades, and the shameful slum conditions of the city's alley housing. [11]

In late 1903 the Associated Charities, with Weller at the helm, invited Jacob Riis to Washington to tour the city's alleys and to testify in Congress. Riis photographed the alleys and alley dwellings with the Capitol in the background and included them in his lecture "How the Other Half Lives," hosted by the Associated Charities at the First Congregational Church downtown. The church was reportedly "filled

An agent of the Associated Charities of Washington, D.C. investigates alley conditions in the early 1900s. (Catholic University of America Archives, Annual Report of the Associated Charities of Washington, D.C., 1902–3.)

and overflowing into G Street." There "every sentence was heard intently" as Riis pronounced DC's alleys as among the worst in the world, "not paralleled by the squalor of New York or London or Paris."[12] In his lecture, Riis urged Congress and President Theodore Roosevelt to act immediately and eliminate alley housing.[13]

Riis's visit inspired a wave of local journalism aimed at exposing the city's alley housing more broadly. Reporters explored the inhabited alleys that were found in all four quadrants of the city. They highlighted the worst of them, singling out Navy Place in Southeast and Dixon Court and Willow Tree Alley in Southwest. In a 1904 headline, the *Washington Times* declared Willow Tree Alley to be "The Toughest Street within the Borders of Washington," while another period account described it as the most "thickly populated" alley in the city, where during the summer its "hundreds of inhabitants swarm outside on their steps to lie in the street, in their efforts to keep cool."[14] According to these accounts, Willow Tree Alley was home to hundreds of the city's poorest residents, including European immigrants and African Americans who lived together "under every circumstance of physical and moral depravity."[15] One police report found fifteen men in a ten-by-fifteen-foot room sleeping on straw covered with vermin.[16]

Just northeast of the Capitol, one reporter described the "winding recesses" of Oriole Court (site of today's Russell Senate Office Building), at the center of which stood "a huge tumbledown stable, around about which the homes of the residents of the alley are ranged in malodorous lines."[17] In Foggy Bottom,

west of the White House, a sociologist reporting on the city's alleys declared the "labyrinthic interior alley" of Snows Court a "festering sore" and called it, together with the adjacent Hughes Court, "one underworld community."[18]

Despite inherent bias found in most of these accounts, the chroniclers called out racial discrimination as a systemic problem in housing the city's mostly Black poor population. African Americans found few housing options in Washington. Many White owners, real estate agents, and others refused to sell or rent to them. While people of all races in the lower income brackets often had no other option than to move into the alleys, African Americans were further denied the better-paying jobs that would eventually enable them to get out of the alleys and into street-facing housing. Mary E. Cromwell, a recorder for the Associated Charities, reported in 1915 that in "Alley K," where she studied approximately sixty family groups, twenty-eight had lived there for ten or more years, twenty-four for twelve or more, and seven for twenty years, and only three for fewer than three years.[19]

Charles Weller and other social and urban reformers continued to push politicians to take up housing reform. In their pleas for alley clearance, they often cited public health concerns: studies invariably found that the infection and death rates of diseases such as pneumonia, tuberculosis, whooping cough, and dysentery were significantly higher for the alley population than for people living in housing facing the street.[20] But these pleas for reform based on health were less out of concern for the alley residents themselves and more about the larger public health fear.[21] In a

The city's alley "slums" stood in close proximity to its grand public buildings and memorials, as illustrated in this 1940s photograph of Dingman Place (between North Capitol Street, New Jersey Avenue, and E and F Streets NW) with the US Capitol to its south. (Library of Congress.)

An alley dwelling in Temperance Court NW (between Twelfth, Thirteenth, T, and U Streets NW) with a sign reading, "2 Room [*sic*] for Rent." (DC Public Library, Star Collection, © *Washington Post*.)

Many of FSA photographer Carl Mydans's photographs of DC's alleys show children posing for pictures along trash-strewn alleys, such as here near the House Office Building (today the Cannon House Office Building). (Library of Congress.)

Washington Post editorial, "Clear Out the Alleys," the reporter condemned the alleys as "wretched slums," a "menace to public health as well as to public order," and "breeding places of disease." The reporter further contended that "Washington is threatened, morally and physically, by their existence."[22] De Graffenried herself concluded that the insanitary condition of the alleys was not only a menace to alley dwellers but also to surrounding residents, as alleys introduced "filth, diseases, and epidemics" into an "otherwise healthy community."[23]

Reformers such as Charles Weller, Jacob Riis, and Mary Clare de Graffenried and the extensive press coverage they provoked succeeded in raising the level of public and political consciousness all the way up to the president's office. In his 1904 Annual Address to Congress, President Roosevelt decried the "hidden residential alleys" as "breeding grounds of vice and decay."[24] He proclaimed that the national capital should be a model city and established the President's Home Commission to look at improving the city's housing failures, naming Charles Weller as its head. Four years later, the commission presented its findings in a four-volume book with reports and recommendations by committees established to study all angles of the housing problem.[25]

Housing reformers, humanitarians, and the President's Home Commission universally agreed that the walled-off aspect of alley life—not the abject poverty or systemic racism that led people to live there—was its most destructive characteristic. For this reason, they all concluded that the elimination of inhabited and hidden alleys was a critical step necessary in addressing the city's housing problem.[26] In her report on the city's alley housing, de Graffenried recommended that the city's inhabited alleys be converted into minor streets. Charles Weller was also a major voice in the movement to convert alleys into minor streets or parks through public and private investments. Weller envisioned alleys being replaced by "garden cities"

Minor Streets

A minor street is a one-block-long street that divides a city block and is narrower than the city streets surrounding the block. A handful of minor streets—essentially through-alleys—were platted as part of the 1791 L'Enfant Plan, but more than one hundred others were introduced during the second half of the nineteenth century. Today minor streets range in width from thirty to seventy-five feet, but in 1894 city regulations required them to be "of a width not less than forty feet or more than sixty feet." Whether part of the L'Enfant Plan or introduced later, minor streets allowed for greater density of development of the city squares.

In the case where little or no development existed on a given square, the conversion of alleys into minor streets held great appeal to land speculators and real estate developers since it allowed for a greater number of buildable lots and thus a greater return on their investments. The resubdivision of squares to replace alleys with minor streets had been taking place since the 1850s, but during the speculative building boom of the 1880s, this occurrence became much more pronounced. The resubdivision of squares with narrower lots and minor streets not only enabled builders to erect more houses for the expanding number of middle-class buyers but it also presented them with the opportunity of self-naming rights (e.g., Corcoran, Hillyer, Willard, and Wiltberger Streets NW) or perhaps of imbuing an upscale quality to the street for marketing purposes (e.g., French and Westminster Streets NW).

During the late nineteenth and early twentieth centuries, humanitarians and housing reformers universally recommended the conversion of the city's inhabited alleys into minor streets. When alleys were already densely built up, however, such conversions proved difficult from both a legal and a financial perspective. As a result, only a few such conversions were carried out by either the public or the private sector.

The Alley Improvement Association, led by Dr. Rev. John Waldron, lobbied the city to improve rather than replace the city's inhabited alleys by bringing sewer, water, and electricity into them. However, Waldron did advocate for replacing the old Civil War–era frame dwellings, like the one shown in this 1943 photograph by FSA photographer Esther Bubley, with brick ones. (Library of Congress.)

abounding with parks and playgrounds and common areas that would encourage more "wholesome lives."[27] Such conversions, however, were both legally challenging and expensive to undertake, and only a few actually came to fruition—for example, that of Willow Tree Alley to Willow Tree Park in Southwest and London Court to Hopkins Place in Southeast.

Where White reformers saw only despair in the inhabited alleys and wanted them replaced with minor streets, many Black leaders were more sanguine and more justly sought to improve the quality of life in the alleys rather than abandon them and their residents. African American leaders such as Dr. Rev. John Milton Waldron, pastor of Shiloh Baptist Church and founder of the nonprofit Alley Improvement Association, provided educational and recreational opportunities for alley residents and lobbied the city for infrastructure improvements. Organized in 1908, the association focused its efforts on thirty selected alleys where it held Sunday school programs and open-air gospel meetings, operated day nurseries, and offered summer outings and vacation Bible school for alley children.[28] Its volunteers provided Thanksgiving and Christmas dinner baskets to alley families and held "clean up" workdays to make physical repairs to neglected alley dwellings. Waldron fully appreciated that the children of the alleys were "bright, apt, well-behaved and trustworthy" but were in need of "everything."[29] He spoke publicly about the deplorable conditions in the alleys and the alley houses, but rather than calling for their condemnation, Waldron encouraged the city to replace the wood-frame dwellings with brick ones, make proper sewer connections, and bring water connections and electricity into the interiors. Waldron favored the formation of a central committee with representatives from all organizations, African American and White, to improve the conditions in the alleys.[30]

Alley Condemnation and Conversion

Congress soon passed several laws to eliminate alley dwellings. In 1906, probably due to the urging of President Roosevelt, Congress passed the Act for the Condemnation of Insanitary Buildings.[31] The act established a board that would identify and condemn insanitary buildings, with the ultimate goal of converting the city's alleys into minor streets or parks. In a two-year period, this law led to the demolition of 545 alley dwellings, including some of the city's "worst shanties."[32] It also provided $78,000 to raze Southwest's Willow Tree Alley houses and create a public park and playground.

The press hailed the 1914 transformation of Willow Tree Alley from "unsightly" structures that housed a "population which numbers nearly a thousand, composed of some of the roughest and toughest element in the city," into a landscaped park.[33] Willow Tree Park and Playground was planted with trees, plants, and flower beds and equipped with a baseball diamond, a wading pool, and playground equipment.[34] As described in the *Sunday Star*, the making of this interior park was "the first work of the kind ever undertaken in this vicinity." In language reflecting the paternalism of the time, the writer continued: "It is an experiment in public welfare activities. . . . Its advocates predict that it will be a powerful and material factor in the movement for the moral improvement and well-being of the community."[35] However well intentioned and successful the creation of Willow Tree Park may have been, such efforts did little to alleviate the city's housing problem, as displaced alley residents were not offered any alternative housing. Most of those forced out simply moved to other equally insanitary alley dwellings or in with family members, exacerbating crowded housing conditions.

In 1913, with her husband's ascent to the presidency and their move to the capital, Ellen Wilson toured several of the city's most populous inhabited alleys. The tour leaders, who were involved in the housing reform movement, brought the First Lady to Willow Tree Alley, then in the process of redevelopment.[36] Impressed by the undertaking, Ellen Wilson became a staunch supporter of the crusade. She then organized tours for congressmen and other politicians and, in her year of ill health just before her death, lobbied for them to act on pending alley eradication legislation. On the day she died, August 6, 1914, she reportedly told her husband, "I should be happier if I knew the alley bill passed." Shortly afterward, Congress passed into law an "Act to provide, in the interest of public health, morals and safety, for the discontinuance of the use as dwellings of buildings situated in the alleys of the District of Columbia," commonly referred to as the "Alley Act" or "Mrs. Wilson's bill."

The Alley Act and a subsequent amendment prohibited the occupation of any structure in any alley not converted to a minor street and called for the complete evacuation of all alley dwellings in the city by July 1, 1918. However, its implementation was delayed due to a World War I housing shortage. To accommodate an influx of war workers, the city needed to retain all of its existing housing, including alley dwellings, and build new temporary shelter. Meanwhile, the only hope for improvement in housing the city's poor rested not with the government but with the efforts of two private philanthropic entities.

Washington's Philanthropic Housing Movement

In three decades of housing reform, legislative efforts focused almost exclusively on the eradication of alley dwellings rather than on safe and affordable housing alternatives. Two private entities set out to fill this void: the Washington Sanitary Improvement Company (WSIC) and its offshoot, the Washington Sanitary Housing Company (WSHC), established in 1897 and 1904, respectively.[37] The philosophies of both companies were rooted in the philanthropic housing movement of nineteenth-century Britain. This movement encouraged speculative builders to invest in housing for the working classes by promising them close-to-market-rate returns, which the organizers achieved through private donations and innovative financing.[38]

Based on this philanthropic housing model, the new WSIC board of directors established its goal of building "wholesome homes" for wage earners at reasonable rates that would provide a modest 5 percent dividend to its investors. It also elected as its first president retired general George Sternberg, a physician who had just completed a distinguished army career and a stint as surgeon general of the United

States. Sternberg's public health work had convinced him that improved housing for the poor was necessary in order to control infectious disease in the general population.[39] At a minimum, sanitary housing would have plumbing for indoor bathrooms and kitchens, electricity, and adequate separation of space for living, eating, and sleeping. The founders' original intention was to redevelop inhabited alleys with sanitary housing for the very poor; however, the cost of assembling the properties and turning the alleys into streets was prohibitive. Instead, the WSIC acquired clusters of unimproved building lots on existing streets on the edges of the city center, where land was accessible to jobs yet still affordable. And the economics of building high-quality housing for the poor did not work for the company. So rather than catering to alley dwellers, the WSIC instead aimed to serve the "better class" of working-class residents.[40]

The company's first project consisted of sixteen two-story brick rowhouses along Bates Street in the Truxton Circle area. These houses, designed by architect James G. Hill, were in fact duplexes with two independent flats—one on each floor—for thirty-two flats in all. The plans provided a three-room model with a living room, a bedroom, a kitchen, and a bathroom and a four-room model with an additional bedroom. Each flat had its own entrance and its own outdoor yard at the rear of the property. And each unit provided running water, indoor plumbing, adequate ventilation, and relief from the crowded living conditions that were endemic to the working-class housing of the time, thus earning them the moniker "sanitary housing."

The first eight houses, completed before the end of 1897, offered the three-room model for monthly rentals of $9.50 and $10 and the four-room one for $12, above the average $9 rent then being charged for the alley dwellings that commonly lacked such amenities. Upon completion of its first Bates Street housing, the company justified its altered mission: "It should be stated that while the original intention was to provide homes for the alley residents and thereby remove the slums, it was considered best to begin this movement by providing improved dwellings for the better class of wage earners, in the belief that houses vacated by them would be rented by the next grade, and so on until the bottom of the ladder was reached."[41]

The WSIC was successful in its initial years and would continue to build housing for several decades, but George Sternberg and others were concerned that it only benefited one segment of the working class. So, in 1904, just after Jacob Riis had toured Washington's alleys and presented his findings to a packed audience, Sternberg and his associates formed the WSHC. The WSHC reduced the paid dividends from 5 percent to 4 percent, enabling the company to lower its rental rates and thus attract alley dwellers and those on the "lower rungs" of the working class.[42] The first WSHC housing was constructed on Van Street SW, immediately across from a windowless row of one-story wooden shacks that had been built as temporary barracks for soldiers during the Civil War. These tiny houses had no water or sewer connections, but, as WSHC had brought water and sewer connections to the street for its own sanitary housing, the owner of the shacks was required by city law to connect those houses to the newly acquired

The WSIC's first group of duplex housing on Bates Street NW in the Truxton Circle neighborhood. Each unit of the company's housing provided running water, indoor plumbing, and adequate ventilation not found in the city's alley dwellings. (DC Public Library, Star Collection, © *Washington Post*.)

city services. Rather than incur such an expense, the owners chose instead to demolish the shacks, providing the WSHC with a partial success story of replacing inferior housing with sanitary housing and offering its residents affordable replacement housing.

With congressional passage of the Board for the Condemnation of Insanitary Buildings Act in 1906 (which would result in the displacement of those living in condemned units), the WSIC and WSHC felt increasing pressure to provide alternative housing for the city's low-income residents. For the next several decades, with no government support, the two philanthropic housing companies worked together to build hundreds of housing units for both African Americans and Whites.[43]

The Alley Dwelling Act of 1934

After fifteen years of legislative inaction since postponement of the 1914 Alley Act, Congress passed, and President Franklin Delano Roosevelt signed into law, the Alley Dwelling Act of 1934. The new law created the Alley Dwelling Authority (ADA), entrusted with ridding Washington of its inhabited alleys. The act established a ten-year time frame in which the ADA was authorized to purchase and/or condemn land and buildings in squares containing inhabited alleys and to redevelop them in a way that would "benefit the neighborhood and the city." To that end, the ADA could either "recondition" existing alley dwellings and open the alleys so the houses were visible from public streets or demolish the dwellings and build new buildings on their sites. The legislation further

established that after July 1, 1944, it would be unlawful to "use or occupy any alley building or structure as a dwelling in the District of Columbia."

The ADA was not only empowered to eliminate alley housing and to find economically and socially viable alternative uses for the city's then more than two hundred inhabited alleys—it was also charged with rehousing displaced residents. This was unlike all previous legislation, which made no such provisions.[44]

Upon passage of the act, John Ihlder, a longtime housing advocate, was named executive director of the ADA, a position he held for a decade. Ihlder was highly knowledgeable and experienced, having been involved with housing in various cities for several decades, and he had a strong moral code with real concern for the future plight of alley residents. After starting in the field with the National Housing Association in New York and before coming to DC, he led housing associations in Pittsburgh, Philadelphia, and Boston. So, when he assumed the mantle as executive director of the ADA, Ihlder clearly understood the dual necessity of both eliminating slum housing and replacing it with better-quality and affordable housing. To that end, he established minimum building standards, including the provision that low-cost housing should have enough open space to allow sufficient light and air, proper sanitation, and an adequate number and proper arrangement of rooms, including a minimum of a living room, a bathroom, and separate bedrooms for the parents, boys, and girls of the family. Ihlder explained that while clearing out the alleys was a legal obligation, providing new and appropriate homes for those forced out was a moral one.[45]

When the legislation was in its planning stages under the Herbert Hoover administration in 1929–30, Ihlder and the politicians sponsoring the bill determined that rehousing alley residents in adequate nearby housing was readily achievable, given the then sufficient supply of housing in the city. By the time the legislation passed in 1934, however, the city was once again facing a severe housing crisis, brought on by the Great Depression and the influx of New Dealers to combat it. Thus, finding adequate housing for displaced alley residents in or near their existing homes became virtually impossible. So, Ihlder shifted the focus of the ADA away from the elimination of alley dwellings and toward the construction of new housing—a trend that intensified after passage of the Housing Act of 1937. This law, commonly called the Wagner-Steagall Act for its congressional sponsors, provided federal subsidies to local public housing agencies, such as the ADA, for the construction of public housing. Although the ADA built some of this new housing in the center city in place of the inhabited alleys, it undertook its most sizable housing projects where land was cheaper, such as east of the Anacostia River.[46] The ADA's first large-scale housing projects, all segregated, included the Frederick Douglass Dwellings, built for African Americans at Twenty-First Street and Alabama Avenue SE, and the Fort Dupont Dwellings, for Whites, at Minnesota Avenue and Ridge Road SE, both in 1940.[47]

As a result of this shift in priorities from demolishing alley dwellings to building low-income housing, the ADA had, by the end of its ten-year mandate in 1944, only "reclaimed" eighteen of the approximately two hundred inhabited alleys that it was meant to eliminate.[48] Of these eighteen reclaimed alleys, the ADA replaced housing with housing in only a few of them; in the others, it built commercial buildings or private garages on the foundations of demolished alley dwellings.[49] John Ihlder explained, "Some of the former slums have been converted to uses other than residential because the character of their neighborhoods has changed in the past two generations."[50] Ihlder often reiterated that the job of the ADA was "to reclaim slums and redevelop them for uses to which their sites are best fitted and to assure adequate supply of good low-rental dwellings."

The first of the ADA's alley rehousing projects, completed in 1936, was the reconfiguration of the I-shaped London Court in square 1023 on Capitol Hill, between Twelfth, Thirteenth, K, and L Streets SE, and its reclamation through the repair of existing dwelling units and the construction of new ones. With funding from the Public Works Administration and labor from the Works Progress Administration, the ADA removed some of the existing alley dwellings and renovated eleven others, bringing them up to the ADA's established and acceptable housing standards. It then built two rows of six new houses, facing each other across a new center lawn. The lawn and walks leading to L Street opened both the existing and new dwellings to the public street, eliminating the blind alley. On the existing houses, the ADA replaced the roofs, doors, windows, and interior flooring and added water closets to rear walls of the houses to replace outhouses in the yards. All the dwellings—old and

As the ADA built new public housing on vacant land in the city's outskirts, it replaced many alley dwellings in the center city with automobile repair facilities, garages, and shops. ADA-constructed automobile-related facilities still stand in several of the city's alleys, including those in Brown's Court SE. These photographs, taken in 1935 and 1936, show workers readying a row of alley dwellings for demolition and the garage that replaced them. The garage, much altered and later converted into a dwelling, still survives in the alley today. (District of Columbia Housing Authority Records, Anacostia Community Museum, Smithsonian Institution.)

new—were hooked up for electricity and rented by the ADA to African Americans. The combined renovation and new construction project was touted as the "first government-built homes for alley dwellers in this city." At its dedication in October 1936, presided over by First Lady Eleanor Roosevelt, the alley was renamed Hopkins Place in honor of Charlotte Everett Wise Hopkins, a civic leader, philanthropist, and proponent of alley eradication who died in 1935.[51] Hopkins is credited with bringing First Lady Ellen Wilson into the campaign to eliminate the

city's alley housing. An open area and playground behind the multistory Hopkins Apartments, built in 1958, now occupies the site of the ADA housing.

In 1937 St. Mary's Court in Foggy Bottom, behind St. Mary's Church on Twenty-Fourth Street between G and H Streets NW, became the second alley rehousing project completed by the ADA. The project, like Hopkins Place the year before, succeeded in rehousing displaced alley residents in the same location, though not without controversy. Before the project started in 1936, the court itself comprised just eight dwellings, but the surrounding streets also contained deteriorated housing, all occupied by African Americans and part of a larger African American neighborhood that had been there for more than half a century. Many of the houses had stood since the Civil War. According to an ADA report, one had been used as a bakery by Union Army troops stationed in the vicinity and the others were built by Blacks after the war, in part with the scrap metal and other materials left by the troops.[52] The court—named for the adjacent St. Mary's Church—was considered "one of the most squalid alleys in the West End."[53] In its stead, the ADA built a two-story, twenty-four-unit apartment building, with two to four rooms per apartment. From the outset, the ADA intended to rent the apartments to the displaced alley residents, all of whom were African American. As the project was nearing completion, however, White developers and residents objected to the plans to rehouse Blacks in the neighborhood. The ADA summed up a number of those arguments:

Negro occupancy would hinder development of the West End; There is a great need for additional housing in the area for Government employees; Additional housing is needed for white students and others who find it advantageous to be near the center of the city; Negroes have no such reason for living in the neighborhood; Loans for white apartments will be made more difficult to secure if the Authority accepts Negroes as tenants for the new building; and Opening of the apartments to Colored tenants will tend to make permanent the Negro population in the West End.[54]

The ADA almost succumbed to the racist pressure, but after criticism and protest by the Lincoln Civic Association, which advocated for Black residents of the West End, the ADA ultimately held firm in its original commitment and opened the apartments to African Americans.[55] Nonetheless, in ensuing years the Lincoln Civic Association criticized the ineffectualness of the ADA, claiming it to have "miserably failed" in its alley reclamation mission of ridding the city of its "slum housing."[56] St. Mary's Court's low-scale housing no longer exists on the site; the former court now provides parking and access for the church and several multistory buildings facing the public streets.

In 1939 the ADA began the most extensive of its alley reclamation projects—the elimination of Navy Place in square 878, between Sixth, Seventh, G, and I Streets SE and its replacement with the new Ellen Wilson Dwellings. Long considered one of the worst and largest of the city's inhabited alleys, Navy Place contained seventy ramshackle dwellings housing two hundred or more families, both Black and White. The eviction process moved slowly, as the ADA was committed to rehousing the residents. "In no case will a dwelling be demolished until the family has found living quarters elsewhere," ADA executive director John Ihlder emphatically informed the press.[57]

In 1941, after the residents were placed in new housing or found it for themselves, Navy Place was redeveloped as the Ellen Wilson Dwellings. The new housing, consisting of 134 units for White low-income residents only, was named in memory of Ellen

The rise of the automobile significantly altered the residential character of the city's inhabited alleys. As seen in this 1950 photograph of Schott's Alley (at the site of the Hart and Dirksen Senate Office buildings on Capitol Hill), half of the alley dwellings had been converted into garages on their first stories. (DC History Center, John P. Wymer Collection, WY 1655.)

Wilson, an ardent housing advocate in her short stint as First Lady. In 2000 a new affordable housing complex known as Townhomes on Capitol Hill replaced the aging Ellen Wilson Dwellings.

Before Ihlder and the ADA were able to accomplish the goal of eradicating all inhabited alleys, however, private efforts to reclaim certain alleys were well underway. These efforts led to a dramatic shift in public policy that allowed for the further retention and renovation of the city's remaining alley dwellings.

CHAPTER 4   Twentieth-Century Alley Renovation

STILL SUFFERING from a Great Depression–era housing shortage, Washington, DC, was, once again, in the throes of a major wartime housing crisis. Thousands of would-be new residents had streamed into the city for federal government and other war-related employment. Before a wartime moratorium on building went into effect during the war, private developers capitalized on the opportunity and began constructing large-scale housing developments, introducing thousands of new dwelling units.

But in a city where housing was still racially segregated, this private-sector housing was largely limited to White occupancy. The federal government constructed war housing for both races on a segregated basis, and as the DC Housing Authority (a more accurate name for the former Alley Dwelling Authority) intensified its campaign of building housing for low-income residents, it reinforced prevailing housing traditions by separating Blacks from Whites in separate housing complexes.[1] As the African American population increased in the wake of the ongoing Great Migration from the South as well as the growth in job

opportunities offered by the expanded federal government, discriminatory housing practices prevailed, and the discrepancy between the number of units of housing available for Blacks and Whites widened. As noted by the biracial Citizens' Committee on Race Relations, Black Washingtonians were "squeezed tighter and tighter into a few little 'islands' within the District."[2] In addition to entire neighborhoods, such as Southwest, these "islands" included the remaining inhabited alleys, still home to thousands of Black residents without the financial means to live anywhere else.

If the Alley Dwelling Authority continued its mission to eliminate the remaining alley dwellings during this crisis, then thousands of residents would be left with nowhere to go. So, Congress extended the ADA's deadline to accomplish its goal, first by two years and then by nine more.[3] The amended act required that all alley dwellings, regardless of condition, be vacated by July 1955. In 1953 the District government's Committee on Discontinuance of Alley Dwellings warned all residents that they had two years to move out of the alleys.

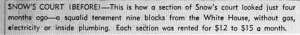

SNOW'S COURT (BEFORE)—This is how a section of Snow's court looked just four months ago—a squalid tenement nine blocks from the White House, without gas, electricity or inside plumbing. Each section was rented for $12 to $15 a month.

SNOW'S COURT (AFTER)—The same row of houses today. Each was stripped to the bare walls and completely modernized. Pastel shutters were added. Iron grill railings will be installed on each set of steps.

These before-and-after photos accompanying a 1953 newspaper article show Black-occupied Snows Court NW in Foggy Bottom as "squalid tenements" and then, after renovation, as "completely modernized" houses for sale to generally higher-income White residents. ("Foggy Bottom Area Gets Face Lifting, *The Sunday Star*, November 8, 1953." DC Public Library, Star Collection ©*Washington Post*.)

To complicate the matter, however, dozens of alley dwellings previously home to low-income African Americans were now home to higher-income White professionals, particularly in Georgetown, Foggy Bottom, and on Capitol Hill.

Confronted with eviction, the new resident-owners heavily invested and comfortably ensconced in their refurbished alley dwellings banded together to protest implementation of the Alley Dwelling Act.

Historic Preservation and Georgetown Alleys

During the post–World War II years, Washington, like all of urban America, witnessed an exodus of White residents to the suburbs. This trend was particularly noticeable after the 1948 Supreme Court decision that ruled racially restrictive covenants were unenforceable. Following this decision, general racial prejudice and the fear of desegregation of their neighborhoods, as well as the lure of new suburban-style housing after years of overcrowding, led White Washingtonians to abandon the city for the close-in and racially homogeneous suburbs of the District in Maryland and Virginia. The growth of the suburbs and the popularity of the automobile prompted changes to the city's urban environment: roadways were widened for cars, buildings were demolished for parking garages and gas stations, and entire neighborhoods were threatened by or destroyed for highway construction. Local residents and real estate investors saw the architectural charm and value of the city's residential building fabric and began the piecemeal renovation of historic buildings in the city's oldest neighborhoods. These small-scale renovation projects, which began principally with street-facing houses, soon expanded into the alleys—a process that would completely upend the socioeconomic character that had marked the alleys since the post–Civil War era.

Georgetown has a long-established and important African American history and presence. Before the founding of the federal city in 1790, one-third of the port town's residents were Black (80 percent enslaved, 20 percent free). Despite some fluctuations over the decades, the percentage of White to African American Georgetown residents would remain remarkably consistent for the next one hundred and twenty years.[4] Before the Civil War, free and enslaved Blacks settled south of M Street along the C&O Canal and near the port, toward the eastern end in the neighborhood bordering Rock Creek, and up and down High Street (today's Wisconsin Avenue).[5] There they established their own residential enclaves, schools, churches, and businesses, contributing to a vibrant African American community that flourished through the decades. The largest was Herring Hill, a fifteen-block area bordering Rock Creek south of P Street and named for the fish that spawned in Rock Creek and served as an important food staple.[6] Though generally in segregated clusters, Blacks and Whites coexisted in proximity to each other in Georgetown throughout the second half of the nineteenth century.

During the early twentieth century, as the industrial operations along the port transitioned away from shipping and milling to meat rendering, incineration, and other more noxious industries, Georgetown became a much less desirable place to live. The new industries brought an influx of menial-labor workers, which led to a shortage of affordable housing. African Americans who had once lived throughout Georgetown were now tightly concentrated in areas with fewer city services, less housing stock, and less desirable surroundings, such as Georgetown's alleys and its old, narrow streets south of M Street.[7]

Beginning in the 1920s and intensifying during the New Deal expansion of the federal government, young White government professionals began investing in the once-fashionable but run-down neighborhood, buying up dilapidated but structurally sound houses, including both large Victorians and more modest ones, and renovating them for their own residency. Many longtime African American property owners willingly sold their houses during this period or were later forced to sell as they could no longer afford the rising property taxes caused by the renovation and improvement of adjacent properties.[8] Those African Americans who rented had no recourse as they were either ousted upon the sale of the house they rented or could ill afford the increasing rental rates of the houses where they were living. In *Black Georgetown Remembered*, Georgetown resident Pauline Gaskin Mitchell recalled, "When the New Dealers came to town and just before that, and when the restoration of Georgetown got well underway, the renters were the first to be ousted because the owners and speculators were determined to take advantage of the pending real estate boom. Many of the homeowners who left Georgetown did so on their own volition. Being unaware of the real value of their property, they were attracted by the seemingly high prices offered."[9]

According to *Black Georgetown Remembered*, five hundred houses in Georgetown were substantially remodeled in the decade from 1935 to 1945.[10] A 1936 *Report from the Conference on Better Housing among Negroes* recognized this deleterious trend on Black Georgetowners: "Since the 1920s, this old port of Washington has been promoted as a quaint, historic, desirable place for white people to live. The dispossession of the Negro resident is part of the redevelopment project, and it is jointly managed by the

city's leading realtors and their allied banks and trust companies."[11]

These discriminatory housing practices and policies were initially limited to the street-facing houses, leaving Black-occupied alley spaces intact well into the 1940s. But as more financially stable White residents filled the street-facing houses, the presence of indigent African Americans in the alleys became increasingly incongruous and undesirable to them. Property owners regularly complained to city authorities about insanitary conditions or noise in the alleys and prevailed on building inspectors to issue infractions in accordance with the 1906 Insanitary Buildings Act. Such complaints ultimately forced the renovation of alley dwellings, contributing to the reordering of Georgetown's alley spaces during this period from Black to White.[12]

As a case in point, in 1949 residents whose houses abutted Bell's Court between Volta Place and Thirty-Third Street NW summoned an inspector from the Board for the Condemnation of Insanitary Buildings to the alley where "bottles, wood and debris littered the narrow court."[13] The court, named in honor of Alexander Graham Bell, who established his laboratory there in the 1880s, was home to forty longtime Black residents. The court historically held a negative reputation, even among Blacks, for the drinking, fighting, card games, and other activities that took place there. In *Black Georgetown Remembered*, Rosemary Wise, a Black former Georgetowner, recalled, "Oh, that is a place . . . you didn't ever go back in there. You just didn't go there period. It was terrible."[14] Based on its inspection, the board declared the court insanitary and ordered the buildings condemned.

Once the houses were condemned, the board required that they be vacated and that the owner, William J. O'Donnell, repair them. According to the city's rent control law, an owner could not evict tenants, but the police could. Two days before Christmas, the police gave O'Donnell's tenants two weeks' notice to leave the premises. The renters, many of whom were longtime residents, told a reporter that they had nowhere to go and little to no money to meet the costs of moving.[15] When four of the residents remained in their condemned homes after the two-week deadline, they were arrested and thrown into jail. Meanwhile, although the board required the owner to make repairs and bring in city services, it provided no protection for the former tenants. Rather than make the repairs himself, O'Donnell sold the houses to Russell Eldridge and Graham Lytle, two Georgetown real estate investors who had already renovated dozens of area homes.[16] Eldridge lived at 1315 Thirtieth Street NW and was credited with the renovation of 125 houses. Graham Lytle lived at 3003 O Street NW and had renovated 60 houses.[17]

As required by city building codes and regulations, the new owners brought plumbing and electricity into the alley and renovated the dwellings. They gutted the houses down to their exterior brick walls and outfitted them with modern kitchens and indoor bathrooms. On the exterior, the new owners painted the dwellings "Williamsburg green" or "Williamsburg off-blue," replaced the windows and doors, and ornamented them with shutters and brass light fixtures, imbuing them with colonial-era charm. The alley itself was repaved and adorned with planted ivy and boxwood. Before putting the houses on the market, the owner renamed the alley and installed iron grillwork at its entrance spelling out its new name: Pomander Walk.

Deemed "unfit for human habitation" just two years earlier, the dwellings, which had rented for $12.50 per month, would be advertised in local newspapers in 1951 for as much as $160 per month. Despite the jump in rates, the renovated dwellings rented quickly, and as reported by an approving and patronizing *Evening Star*, they were occupied by "an entirely new generation of renters. . . . Among them will be Navy and Army officers, a State Department official, a writer, a secretary from the Swedish Embassy and an official of the Defense Production Authority. . . . The area has gone white, and the little colored colony has found quarters elsewhere."[18]

The former tenants, many of whom had lived in Bell's Court for more than a decade, dispersed to other areas of the city. Three families moved to Dingman Place, an alley in Northeast on Capitol Hill that the *Evening Star* described as "damp, cold, muddy and full of insects and rats."[19] Another resident moved to the 400 block of Ridge Street NW, where she paid $67.50 in rent in addition to utilities for a residence the same size as her Bell's Court house. Still, Russell Eldridge's wife, who helped in the renovation project of Bell's Court, pronounced assuredly, "Moving was really a blessing in disguise. For they were overcrowded into these formerly rat-ridden small homes. They have now gotten new homes that are clean, modern and convenient. They now have baths and other facilities that

Condemned Slum in Georgetown Alley Goes High Hat as Pomander Walk

In 1951, after the ten houses of Bell's Court in Georgetown, formerly home to low-income African American residents, were renovated, the owner renamed the alley "Pomander Walk" in an attempt to shed its association with the former "alley slum" of Bell's Court. (DC Public Library, Star Collection, © *Washington Post*.)

are required by District regulations or have moved out into the suburbs where their children will have a better chance."[20]

Other Georgetown alleys saw similar conversions, including East Place (between Twenty-Fifth, Twenty-Sixth, P, and Q Streets), Poplar Alley (between Twenty-Seventh, Twenty-Eighth, O, and P Streets), and the ten-foot-wide Cherry Hill and Cecil Alleys in the industrial section of Georgetown below the canal. In 1951 the then owner of the twenty-six houses lining Cherry Hill and Cecil Alleys began to

sell them one by one to individual buyers, displacing some 150 tenants in the process. The purchasers—middle- and professional-class Whites—renovated the houses for their own occupation.[21]

Outside of Georgetown, beginning in the late 1940s and early 1950s, several other alley renovation projects were also underway. Typical of the reporting at that time, the local press generally lauded these alley improvements, focusing particularly on Terrace Court and Library Court on Capitol Hill and Snows Court, Green's Court, and Hughes Court in Foggy

A present-day image of Terrace Court NE, once condemned as an "unsightly slum." (Photo by author, 2021.)

Bottom. In one of the first instances of alley restoration, six buyers purchased eight alley dwellings in Terrace Court, located at the center of square 759 between Second, Third, East Capitol, and A Streets NE, immediately east of the Supreme Court Building. The new owners—well-to-do Whites—brought electricity and water into the alley, demolished the privies, and began to upgrade the modest dwellings. As reported by the *Evening Star* in 1947, the exterior walls were painted white, shutters were added, along with lantern-type lights, and "a Colonial atmosphere will predominate" in the "once unsightly slum."[22]

In Foggy Bottom the local press highlighted the renovation of several groups of alley dwellings, including twenty-six "ramshackle" row houses in Snows Court, a row of houses in Hughes Court, and several in Green's Court.[23] In 1953 Eleanor Lansing Dulles, sister of Secretary of State John Foster Dulles, bought three houses in Green's Court and began fixing them up. Joseph Robitscher, a George Washington University medical student and his wife Jean, a former newspaper and magazine writer, undertook several rows of houses in Snows Court and collaborated with another couple, Ben and Dorothy Burch, on the renovation of houses in Hughes Court.[24] In each of these cases, the press noted that the buyers planned to renovate and then sell the houses to individual buyers, rather than put them on the rental market. As part of the process, they brought in gas, electricity, and indoor plumbing, repointed and painted the brick walls, and replaced the windows and roofs.[25] In describing the Robitschers' renovation of a row of seven dwellings in Snows Court, the *Evening Star* recounted, "The 93-year old dwellings, which had deteriorated into

Snows Court NW today. (Photo by author, 2014.)

scarcely more than hovels, each occupied by 10 or 12 unfortunate Negroes, were stripped back to the bare walls. All interior partitions were removed, and new flooring was laid over the old."[26] The paper, which had just a few years earlier referred to Snows Court as a "festering sore," now extolled the buildings' charm, found particularly in its window shutters and the "authentic Williamsburg" paint colors.

Once ensconced in their renovated dwellings, the new residents, like the owner of Bell's Court-*cum*-Pomander Walk, petitioned the city to change the names of their alleys to lessen associations with their past.[27] In 1947 the residents of Terrace Court lobbied unsuccessfully for it to be called "Little Street," but shortly thereafter the District commissioners voted to allow "alley-dwellers to name, at their pleasure, the alleys in which they dwell, so long as they pay for appropriate street signs."[28] In response, residents of the unnamed renovated alley near Third and A Streets SE called it Library Court due to its proximity to the Library of Congress, while those in Foggy Bottom's Hughes Court voted simply to become Hughes

Children running through Poplar Alley in Georgetown before the alley conversion pushed out its Black residents. See page 17 for a present-day photograph. (DC Public Library, Georgetown, Peabody Room.)

Mews because, as reported by the *Washington Post*, "it sounds rather more picturesque" and because of the alley's resemblance to the "many streets so designated in England."[29] In Georgetown, in addition to Bell's Court becoming Pomander Walk, Cherry Hill Alley became Cherry Hill Lane, and Poplar Alley became Poplar Street. On Capitol Hill, Schott's Alley was renamed Schott's Court as it was being transformed from "a rat-infested, overcrowded and rowdy alley to an L-shaped row of luxury type apartments."[30]

In 1953 the District Committee on Discontinuance of Alley Dwellings began to warn residents of alley dwellings that they had two years to move or be evicted so that all buildings, irrespective of their condition, could be demolished. By then, some sixty to seventy alley dwellings in Georgetown, Foggy Bottom, and Dupont Circle and on Capitol Hill had been renovated, and dozens more were just getting started.[31] In public hearings and published opinion pieces,

residents and owners of renovated alley dwellings protested vehemently. They argued that demolition was unnecessary because they had achieved the "spirt of the law" by accomplishing slum clearance through their private efforts. One opinion piece by Ella Dakin Brown and Olga Jamison Brown of Terrace Court argued that they "took the initiative and with private capital transformed a neglected, ugly area into a picturesque, modern, healthful community." Furthermore, they contended, "grave injustice will be done us, not to mention the hardships imposed, should we be forced to vacate our modern, comfortable little homes, those to stand empty, deteriorating, becoming a festering wound, inviting crime and violence to take over a now orderly community."[32]

Unmoved, the District continued to pursue the letter of the law. Residents of renovated alley dwellings responded by banding together as the Washington Court Dwellers Association, the Progressive Citizens of Georgetown, Capitol Hill Southeast Citizens Association, the Cherry Hill Citizens Association, and other entities.[33] Together they declared that about two million dollars had been invested in the rehabilitation projects and about one hundred out of nine hundred remaining alley dwellings were renovated or were in the process. In testimony before the District commissioners in September 1953, a representative from the Capitol Hill Southeast Citizens Association argued that the alley houses in Southeast were "works of art," and the Washington Court Dwellers Association contended that it was not the intent of Congress, back in 1934, to destroy modern homes, occupied by "respectable people," when it passed the Alley Dwelling Act. An attorney representing the Washington Court Dwellers Association testified that to ban occupancy of all alley dwellings would be a "violation of the Constitution and would amount to a taking of property without due process."[34] Needless to say, such arguments were absent when the low-income African American alley residents were being forcibly removed as part of the ADA's mission to eradicate the city's alley dwellings.

In May 1955 the owners' lobbying paid off. Just before the citywide ban was to go into effect, Congress repealed the Alley Dwelling Act. Renovated alley dwellings could remain intact. To celebrate the victory, alley house owners in Georgetown's newly named Cherry Hill Lane held a "dancing in the street" party with a professional square- and round-dance director and caller. The ten-foot-wide streets were decorated with colorful Japanese lanterns, and food and punch were plentiful.[35]

Repeal of the Alley Dwelling Act in 1955 not only allowed for the retention of existing alley dwellings but also opened the door for the construction of new dwellings in the city's alleys. Some of these new residences, like the large freestanding dwellings on F Street Terrace NE on Capitol Hill shown here, and Scott Place NW in Georgetown, were not so much alley dwellings as sizable, detached houses that were built along alleys. (Photo by author, 2014.)

The act's repeal not only allowed for rehabilitated alley dwellings to remain in place but it also opened the door for the construction of new alley dwellings. Within a year, developers looked to alleys within the city's historic neighborhoods as an opportunity for new, upscale residential infill. Once completed, some of these new residences, such as those on F Street Terrace NE on Capitol Hill and Scott Place NW in Georgetown were not so much alley dwellings as sizable detached houses oriented to face the alleys.[36]

Others, such as the pair of dwellings at 2719 and 2721 Poplar Street NW, built just months after the repeal of the ban, were not much wider than their nineteenth-century predecessors, though they were one story taller and accommodated automobile garages in the first story. In Brown's Court SE on Capitol Hill, a row of alley dwellings built after the 1955 repeal are no larger than their historic neighbors but are executed in a wholly contemporary styling that sets them apart.

Almost immediately the construction of new houses in the city's alleys was met with controversy.[37] In May 1956, when a developer proposed to build six houses along the narrow, fourteen-foot-wide Orchard Alley within Thirtieth, Thirty-First, P, and Q Streets in Georgetown as part of the subdivision of a historic tract of land, area residents responded with angry disbelief that dwellings could be built in the narrow alley behind their houses. The residents on all sides of Orchard Alley challenged the city's regulations, arguing that Orchard Alley was too narrow and that the proposed houses would cause a bottleneck and, more important, posed a fire threat to adjacent properties.[38] The District Zoning Commission took up the case, and although it could not overturn the congressional repeal, it agreed that Orchard Alley was too narrow and reestablished the 1892 regulation banning any new construction in alleys less than thirty feet wide.[39] Ultimately the developer was able to build the houses along Orchard Alley because he acquired an additional sixteen feet as part of the subdivision of the larger tract and was thus able to convert the fourteen-foot alley into a thirty-foot-wide one.[40]

Shortly after construction began on the Orchard Alley (renamed Orchard Lane) houses in July 1956, another developer proposed to build a new thirty-foot-wide alley within the same interior square and build nineteen new houses. Again residents objected—to no avail—claiming that the proposed development would make Georgetown overcrowded.[41] Within a year, the developer carved out the new West Lane Keys and began building houses to face it. In January 1959 he advertised the one yet-unsold house, highlighting it as one of "Georgetown's most discussed group of federal town houses [with] some of the finest features to afford one exquisite and comfortable living."[42]

While the twentieth-century renovation of alley dwellings in Georgetown, Foggy Bottom, and on Capitol Hill preserved some historic alleys and alley dwellings into the present (and added new ones), alley dwellings in Southwest, downtown, and neighborhood commercial areas did not fare so well. In Southwest the blighted and low-income row-house neighborhood with its many alleys was radically transformed when, beginning in the 1950s, the District of Columbia Redevelopment Land Agency began implementing one of the earliest and most ambitious urban renewal projects in the country. An initial plan for the redevelopment of the area called for the preservation and rehabilitation of nearly half the area's housing stock by weaving new construction into the existing urban fabric.[43] As finalized, the plan instead resulted in the redevelopment of the entire neighborhood, replacing its traditional street plan and rowhouses with superblocks to accommodate high-rise apartments, townhouses, a shopping center with a theater, federal and local government office

This group of alley dwellings at 603–611 Brown's Court SE replaced a row of nineteenth-century alley dwellings that stood on the site until around 1960. The row of dwellings had escaped demolition by the ADA in the 1930s because they had been converted into garages. (Photo by author, 2021.)

buildings, public parks, and a waterfront revitalized as an entertainment destination, all catering to a higher-income residential base. As part of this urban clearance plan, the historic rows of housing lining the L'Enfant Plan streets and alleys, the vast majority of which lacked indoor toilets, electricity, and central heating, were vacated and demolished, displacing some twenty-three thousand residents, two-thirds of whom were African American.[44] In the spring of 1954, the demolition of Dixon Court and its alley dwellings, marking the first phase of the plan to be undertaken,

was hailed by the *Washington Post*, which deemed Dixon Court "a sore spot of crime, illegitimacy, refuse and disordered lives."[45]

The urban renewal plan intended to rehouse residents in some of this new housing, and to that end several low-income and public housing complexes were indeed constructed. For the most part, however, market forces won out, and the new apartment buildings and townhouses largely catered to a wealthier and Whiter population. Most of the former residents of Southwest never returned.

Despite the decades-long efforts of humanitarians and government policies to eradicate alley dwellings, it was ultimately other political, economic, and social forces that contributed instead to the gradual decline in the number of inhabited alleys in the city. The widespread construction of streetcar lines in the late nineteenth century and the introduction of the automobile in the early twentieth century allowed for greater population dispersal beyond the city's core, thereby reducing the pressure to build housing in the alleys. These new modes of transportation spawned the development of new building types, such as garages, which in turn led to the removal or repurposing of alley dwellings. Similarly, new types of commerce and industry inspired the growth of new building types, all of which vied for space in the alleys of an increasingly urban city center.

CHAPTER 5   Commerce and Industry in the Alleys

WASHINGTON'S OCCUPIED ALLEYS may have been hidden from public view, but in the late nineteenth and early twentieth centuries they teemed with activity beyond the residential. The comings and goings of horses and workers and the greater cacophony of machinery and animals competed with the joyful sounds of children playing just as the noxious smells of iron being welded and horse manure compromised the sweet aromas of baking bread. Alleys were a vital component of the city's existence, where residents shared their spaces with horse stables and carriages, workshops, warehouses, manufacturing plants, storage facilities, coal yards, woodsheds, and more.

Bakeries and Bottling

Commercial and semi-industrial businesses such as bakeries, breweries, dairies, and bottling plants were major employers for city residents during the late nineteenth and early twentieth centuries. Such businesses were particularly robust in the alleys along Seventh Street NW , the city's primary commercial corridor. Since the early years of the city's

establishment, Seventh Street provided the principal route into and out of Washington. It carried people—farmers, wholesalers, merchants, and market-goers—from the rural outskirts directly to Center Market with its stalls and wagons at Seventh Street and Pennsylvania Avenue NW (now site of the National Archives). Northern Liberty Market, first at Mount Vernon Square and after 1874 at Fifth and K Streets NW, offered a smaller venue along the route. Here, the corridor was lined with stores and restaurants, and adjacent streets hosted trade stores, supply shops, and retail and wholesale outfits offering an array of goods and services. Tradespeople, artisans, and entrepreneurial residents, including recent immigrants, many of whom were German or Italian, and newly emancipated African Americans, found work in existing businesses or established their own, adding to the vibrancy of the area.

Prather's Alley, in the square between Fourth, Fifth, I, and K Streets NW, just one block south of the Northern Liberty Market and just east of the Seventh Street commercial corridor, offered tradespeople and entrepreneurs the perfect opportunity to

Established in 1889, Simpson's Walker Hill Dairy occupied an extensive array of buildings along Prosper Alley (today an unnamed alley) on Capitol Hill between Seventh, Eighth, E, and G Streets SE. One of the alley's buildings housed the company's oxen that pulled heavy wagons filled with cans of milk from Union Station, where it had been brought from outlying farms. Once in the alley, the milk was bottled and then delivered, first by horse-drawn wagons and later by trucks, to grocery stores, hotels, and restaurants across the city. (DC Historic Preservation Office; photo by Jim Simpson.)

capitalize on the post–Civil War building boom and ready commercial market. The area was only sparsely developed in the years leading up to and immediately after the Civil War, but once the Northern Liberty Market moved from Mount Vernon Square two blocks east to a new and vast market building at Fifth and K Streets NW, Prather's Alley quickly attracted a network of businesses catering to the needs of the growing city. By the early twentieth century, Prather's Alley was brimming with a bakery, a bottling plant, a blacksmith shop, stabling and warehousing facilities, and residents who shared the alley with the emerging commercial enterprises.

One of these—an extensive bakery complex including ovens, flour storage warehouses, a wagon house, and stables, established by German baker Charles

This photograph of Nayle's (or Nailor's or Naylor's) Alley, once found between Fourth, Fifth, K, and L Streets NW, reveals the variety of activities historically found in the city's alleys. On the left of the photograph are garages, former stables, and warehouses. Along the right side is the Purity Ice Company plant, two-story alley dwellings, and garages. In the center background is the side elevation of the Northern Liberties Market. The Alley Dwelling Authority took this picture in 1936 during its campaign to eradicate substandard alley dwellings. Today this alley no longer exists, but the alley to its south, Prather's Alley, does, along with several of its historic alley buildings. (National Capital Housing Authority.)

In 1871 a group of market vendors formed the Northern Liberty Market Company and built a massive brick-and-iron market building at Fifth and K Streets NW. The market, now demolished, housed 284 vending stalls and spurred the growth of a sizable mercantile community in the surrounding streets and alleys into the mid-twentieth century. (DC History Center, General Photographic Collection.)

Schneider—filled the eastern end of the alley. Every morning before the light of day, some fifty workers streamed into the alley to begin the daily process of stoking the ovens to nourish the city's populace. Dozens of those workers disappeared into the various bakery buildings to knead, weigh, and mold the dough and tend the ovens that produced twenty-five thousand loaves of bread a day, but many others filled the alley itself, offloading flour to the warehouse or hitching the horses and loading the baked goods into the company's twenty-five delivery wagons.[1]

In addition to this immense bakery enterprise, John J. Bowles, owner of a dairy farm in Rockville,

Maryland, opened a milk bottling plant in the alley. Bowles had been operating a small dairy shop, J. J. Bowles Jersey Dairy, on H Street NW, but around the turn of the twentieth century, he wanted to grow his business and saw an opportunity near Northern Liberty Market and the busy and well-positioned Prather's Alley. Bowles moved into a house at 458 K Street NW and at its rear built a two-story brick bottling plant in the alley. Every day, milk from Bowles's Jersey herd was brought into the city and delivered to Prather's Alley where it was processed, bottled, and then delivered to customers by a squadron of horse-drawn wagons, also stabled in the alley.

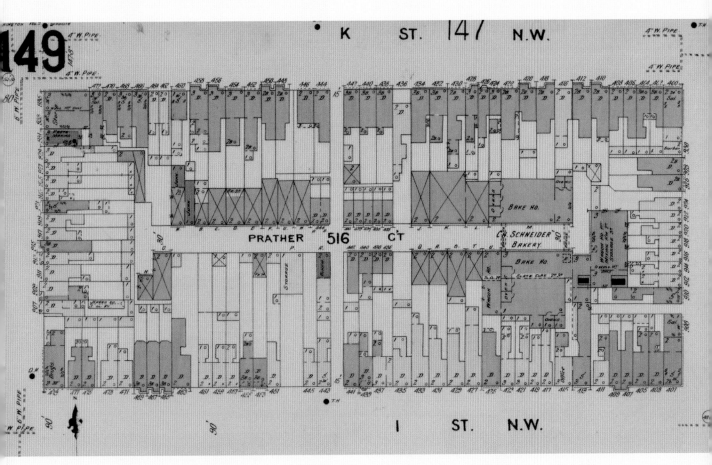

This detail of a 1904 map shows Prather's Alley NW and its wide mix of building uses. Dwellings (marked "D") and stables (marked "X") coexisted with a bottling plant, warehouses, and a bakery. (Library of Congress.)

To help staff his bottling plant, Bowles brought workers in from the country and housed them in the three-story apartment building at 460 K Street NW that he constructed immediately in front of his bottling plant and next to his own house.[2] Bowles maintained his business for years, competing with dozens of other dairies across the city before merging with Simpson's Walker Hill Dairy on Seventh Street SE on Capitol Hill in the 1920s. Together the dairies delivered about five thousand gallons of milk daily to stores, hotels, and lunch-counter restaurants."[3]

As Bowles's business was expanding and Prather's Alley was already filled with the activities of baking and bottling, William Beuchert, a former route salesman for Charles Schneider, vied with his fellow German and former boss for space in the alley. Around the turn of the twentieth century, Beuchert established a commercial stable in Prather's Alley, and then in 1912 he built a blacksmith shop for horseshoeing and wagon repair and a few years later an attached warehouse on the south side of the alley.

Within a month of the completion of the blacksmith shop, the *Washington Post* opined that "the time is not far off when the horse-drawn vehicle will be as great a curiosity as the cross-town streetcar of New York" and hailed the truck as the "surer, cheaper, better means of conducting business."[4] Four years later, and as if on cue, Beuchert erected a garage for the repair of automobiles in front of his alley-facing blacksmith shop.[5] The repair shop, Central Auto Works, later became an artist's studio and gallery (Gold Leaf Studios) and is now the lobby and retail space

A circa 1922 photo of a Walker Hill Dairy delivery truck in Prosper Alley SE on Capitol Hill. (Library of Congress.)

This photo taken in 2004 shows a former blacksmith shop (left) and two warehouses (right) in Prather's Alley NW, surviving historic commercial buildings in the once densely packed alley in today's Mount Vernon Triangle neighborhood. See page 120 for a present-day photo. (Photo by D. P. Sefton, 2004.)

of a multistory condominium that also incorporates Beuchert's former blacksmith shop and warehouse.

Farther north from Prather's Alley, just inside the city's original boundary at today's Florida Avenue (historically called Boundary Street), Wiltberger Street and its adjacent alleys emerged as another center of the city's baking community. In 1857 real estate speculator Charles Wiltberger had cut the thirty-foot-wide minor street through the square with two ten-foot-wide alleys running parallel to it on either side. For the next decade or so, the minor street became home to two-story frame dwellings and their occupants, while the flanking alleys provided service sheds and stables. The sweet aroma of baking bread began to emanate

from the alleys during the post–Civil War economic boom when Bavarian-born baker Charles Specht built a bake oven along the west side of Wiltberger Alley and opened his bakery shop in front of it at 1811 Seventh Street NW. For years Specht worked his trade in isolation until he was joined, and later succeeded, by two other bakers, also of German descent—Michael Holzbeierlein and Peter Michael Dorsch.

Over the decades, Holzbeierlein's and Dorsch's bakeries transformed the quiet residential area into a major center of the baking industry that not only dominated the interior of the square but also exerted an imposing presence along the 600 block of S Street NW.

During the early twentieth century, Dorsch's and Holzbeierlein's bakeries, both of which began in the alleys, expanded their operations into Wiltberger Street, a minor street cutting through the square bounded by Sixth, Seventh, S, and T Streets NW. The former Holzbeierlein Bakery, the red brick building to the left of the photo, was recently redeveloped into condominiums, while Dorsch's White Cross Bakery across the street and facing S Street (not shown in photo), was converted into the Mark Wonder Bread Factory Flex Office Space. (Photo by author, 2021.)

Dorsch's White Cross Bakery

At the age of nineteen, Peter Michael Dorsch, the son of a Bavarian immigrant shopkeeper and his wife, became proprietor of a baking business at Third and I Streets SW. Dorsch ran the bakery, Dorsch Brothers Bakery, with the help of his three brothers, a sister-in-law, and his parents and within a few years moved his store to Georgetown. But when fellow Bavarian baker Charles Specht was looking to sell his Wiltberger Street bakery in 1905, Peter Dorsch seized the opportunity. After purchasing the bakery and ovens, he and his extended family moved into the two-story shop on Seventh Street NW with the bake ovens at the rear.

Peter Dorsch's expansion of his bakery business coincided with the early stages of the sanitary food movement. Upton Sinclair's novel *The Jungle* (1906), which had exposed Americans to the inhumane and insanitary working conditions of the country's meatpacking industry, led Progressive Era reformers and the press to challenge traditional handmade manufacturing and production processes of other food products, such as bread. In one such article, the *New York Times* extolled the newer bakeries and their automated equipment that produced a uniform product "untouched by human hands."[6] In this climate of sanitary concerns, Peter Dorsch responded. He upgraded his existing bakery buildings along Wiltberger Street and alleys and erected a new and larger factory facing the 600 block of S Street NW with machinery and automated services. The new building's decorative features—white crosses in the central pediment and cornice—advertised his company's name, Dorsch's White Cross Bakery, subliminally instilling confidence in the sanitary quality of the company's baked goods.[7] According to the *Evening Star*, the new 1915 bakery building's first floor contained "two continuous ovens of the latest type" for bread baking and an oven for baking cakes on the second floor.[8] When the plant started, it produced two to three hundred loaves of bread daily. By 1922, after a major

In a strategic marketing move addressing the public's concern over food sanitation, baker Peter Dorsch named his business Dorsch's White Cross Bakery and built a new bakery building in 1915, introducing white terra cotta crosses into its facade as a branding logo. The crosses, similar to that of the American Red Cross, imparted a sense of cleanliness and healthfulness important to the Progressive Era consumer. (Photo by author, 2021.)

addition, it was turning out one hundred thousand loaves daily, in addition to forty varieties of cakes.[9]

In 1925 the Continental Baking Company, famous for its presliced Wonder Bread and Hostess-brand cake products, moved into the DC market and in 1936 purchased Dorsch's White Cross Bakery. The company operated the former Corby Bakery on Georgia Avenue as its principal Wonder Bread factory, while converting the White Cross Bakery into production of its Hostess cake products. Recently renovated, the former White Cross Bakery building complex offers flex work space to city residents.

Manufacturing and Warehousing

In addition to dairy bottling plants and bakeries, other consumer-based industries found manufacturing and warehousing quarters in the city's alleys. Some of these were small, independent businesses whose buildings still stand, such as that of a cabinetmaker in Essex Court in old downtown who built models for those seeking patents at the nearby US Patent Office, the G. W. Mason Carriage Works in Georgetown, a blacksmith shop in Prather's Alley NW, and even a testing lab, the Gyro Motor Company, on Girard Street in Columbia Heights, established by entrepreneur Emile Berliner for his experimentation with and fabrication of the rotary engine. However, of all the different types of buildings constructed in the city's alleys to house the wide range of activities that took place there, the most common of all was the horse stable.

Stables

As Washington grew from a sparsely developed city before the Civil War to a burgeoning metropolis in the mid to late nineteenth century, horse stables became indispensable buildings to house the city's growing horse population. Extensive stabling facilities provided shelter for the city's workhorses involved in the distribution of goods and city services such as hauling coal and trash, pulling fire apparatuses, and delivering milk and more. Large livery stables, such as McCaully's Tally Ho Stables in Naylor Court, Nash's Stables in Blagden Alley, and Proctor's Stables downtown, all of which still stand, were built to house

horses and carriages for hire and to board privately owned horses. Liveries provided a variety of other services, including shoeing, wagon rental, and machinery repairs. Individuals with the means to own their own horses and/or carriages built smaller, private stables at the rear of the houses along the alleys throughout the interior of the city squares.

Private Stables

In the last decades of the nineteenth century, thousands of private stables—of which several hundred survive in various stages of repair—lined the city's alleys.[10] While many of these now-obsolete buildings are being creatively adapted for new uses as residences, restaurants and cafés, yoga studios, and other retail spaces, the stable as a building type remains readily recognizable for its original intended use.

The typical urban stable is generally an unassuming building characterized by its functional qualities and not so much by architectural style or ornament. Features such as wide carriage door openings on the ground story and hayloft doors on the second identify the buildings' historical stable use. Wooden beams protruding from just above the hayloft opening allowed for a pulley system to hoist feed to the loft level for storage. Workers would pitch the hay from the loft down wooden chutes leading directly into bins for the horses to feed on.

Horse stall windows are another key architectural feature of stables. These small windows are often found along the side wall of the stable building, indicating the location and number of horse stalls inside. Although

This former stable at 1315 Naylor Court NW, built in 1899, was the center of delivery operations for E. J. Adams, a successful grocer whose sign has been resurrected on the side of the building. Now a residence, it served a variety of uses throughout its history, including being home to a woodworking shop that made artificial limbs during World War II. (Photo by author, 2021.)

James Fraser built this stable in the alley behind his residence at 1701 Twentieth Street NW in Dupont Circle. Both the house and stable were designed by noted local architects Hornblower & Marshall in the early 1890s. The stable has been converted into a private residence. (DC Historic Preservation Office.)

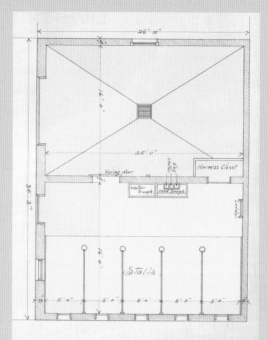

This architectural plan for a stable and carriage house for the first floor of a DC police station shows stalls for five horses and an adjacent carriage room with a harness closet. The second floor (plan not shown) housed the hayloft over the carriage room and a hostler's room above the stalls. (DC Department of General Services, Municipal Buildings Drawings Collection.)

The typical nineteenth-century urban stable, like this one in the alley behind the 1300 block of T Street NW, featured wide doors on the ground level to accommodate horses and carriages and a loft door above. The wooden block protruding from above the loft door historically held an apparatus for lifting hay or other feed to the loft for storage. (Photo by author, 2021.)

Most private stables in DC were simple utilitarian brick structures that lacked architectural ornamentation. This stable at 1619 (Rear) Connecticut Avenue is exceptional for its decorative brickwork and terra cotta detailing. (DC Historic Preservation Office, 2014.)

not all horse stalls had windows, historical treatises on stable construction highly recommended them for the health of the horses: "A horse's mind is kept keener when he is thus allowed to see passing objects than when tied against a black wall; and his eyesight is certainly not strained as is that of a horse which is taken from a dark stall into the bright daylight."[11]

Wealthy Washingtonians built commodious and architecturally distinctive stables or carriage houses that often complemented their opulent mansions. In 1901 Thomas Francis Walsh did just that when he concurrently commissioned the design and construction of his lavish mansion at 2020 Massachusetts Avenue NW (the present-day Indonesian embassy) and a private carriage house and stable in a nearby alley. Walsh, who had emigrated penniless from Ireland in 1869, made a fortune in the post–Civil War gold rush. Decades later, Walsh lost it all in the economic panic of 1893, but within just a few years he made it all back after opening the Camp Bird Mine in Ouray, Colorado—a highly productive gold and silver mine. After selling the mine for $5.2 million (valued close to $1.5 billion dollars in 2022), he moved to DC with his family to invest in real estate and to indulge in the extravagant lifestyle of Washington and its active social scene. He hired New York architect Henry Anderson to design a sixty-room mansion complete with grand staircase and open foyer reminiscent of an ocean liner, a music room with a pipe organ, and a ballroom, all to flaunt his wealth and to accommodate his desire for lavish entertaining. Walsh complemented his mansion with a well-appointed stable and carriage house in an adjacent alley west of his mansion. Designed by local builder Lemuel Norris and

This onetime stable, located at the rear of 1511 Twenty-Second Street NW, was built by Thomas Walsh, whose extravagant mansion stood nearby at 2020 Massachusetts Avenue NW. It is currently home to a custom framing and fine art gallery. (Photo by author, 2021.)

featuring fanciful Flemish gables, it is notably exuberant compared to most other stables in DC. Walsh died within a decade of building his Washington mansion, but his wife, Carrie, who outlived her husband by many years, continued to live there. During World War I, she converted the house into a garment factory and until her death in 1932 was said to have been one of the last residents of the city to keep a carriage in a carriage house.[12] During World War II, the Walshes' daughter, Evelyn Walsh McLean renovated the stables for use as a club for women war workers.

What's in a Name?

The term "stable" describes a building in which horses are housed, harnessed, and fed. The term "carriage house" refers to a building in which carriages are stored, washed, and maintained and where coachmen, grooms, and stablemen reside. Often the stable and carriage house were connected or combined into a single building and were interchangeably referred to as either stable or carriage house. To further complicate the distinction, many urban stables did not actually house horses but were strictly meant for carriages, as horses were often boarded off-site at livery stables. The presence of stall windows in a stable provides good evidence that the building was intended for the housing of horses.

Liveries

Maintaining a horse not only required the space to board the animal but also time or staff to feed, groom, exercise, and care for it. As an alternative to private ownership, and for a fee, of course, commercial livery stables would both board a privately owned horse or hire out horse and carriage as necessary. From the Civil War era until the early twentieth-century advent of the automobile, several dozen privately run commercial stables could be found across the city. The most public of commercial livery stables typically fronted public streets, but others were located within the city's private network of alleys. In the last decades of the

nineteenth century, Benjamin F. McCaully, considered an authority on thoroughbred horses and well regarded for his deep knowledge of and high-quality care of horses, operated the city's largest livery in the middle of Naylor Court.

McCaully's Tally Ho Stables—a massive commercial stable constructed in 1883 and presently home to the DC Archives—was in its heyday, according to the local press, "the largest and finest livery stable in this part of the country."[13] The operation comprised a 100-by-95-foot building that contained a carriage house on the ground floor and stalls for seventy-five to two hundred horses, according to differing accounts, and a harness room above reached by a hydraulic elevator. McCaully had an imposing fleet of three hundred carriages to be chosen from, including "landaus, coupes Victorias, wagonette surreys, buggies and saddle horses," which could be rented by the hour, month, or year.[14]

Tally Ho Stables had a blacksmith on the premises and offered horseshoeing, carriage painting, and repair services along with an automatic, steam-driven coach cleaner. McCaully was touted for operating an efficient and well-run business where he could "turn out in a moment's notice" a "perfectly appointed equipage, the last speck of dust having been removed from the silken linings and glossy varnish, and the least atom of corrosion displaced from the silver mountings of the trappings and the glittering buttons of the livery."[15] For decades Naylor Court was abuzz with human and equine activity as patrons came into the alley to rent or return horse or carriage. There carriage drivers and hostlers moved horses and carriages into

Wilbur Nash's commercial livery in Blagden Alley NW, shown here, and the Tally Ho Stable building in the adjacent Naylor Court still stand. (Photo by author, 2021.)

and out of the stables, workers painted and repaired carriages, and the blacksmith cleaned and shod the horses' hooves.

When McCaully entered the livery business in 1887, he joined an already active enterprise in the city that boasted dozens of commercial stabling facilities. A. R. Fowler had been engaged in boarding and renting horses and carriages since before the Civil War and continued to operate his livery stable, which he advertised heavily, for decades. Wilbur Nash, an entrepreneur who secured sizable federal government contracts during his career, was late on the scene when in 1909 he built a large commercial stable in Blagden Alley just one block south of McCaully's.[16] Five years later, just as the garage was beginning to supplant the stable, Nash built a second stable on Snows Court—still standing but vacant—at the center of the Foggy Bottom alley.

While essential for the transportation needs of the city's residents, these large-scale accommodations did not always do well for the horses. In the days of kerosene lanterns and candles, stables with their stalls full of straw bedding and their lofts full of hay feed were serious firetraps. A few months after the end of the Civil War, A. R. Fowler's frame livery stable on New York Avenue near Fifteenth Street NW caught fire, destroying his nineteen horses as well as considerable property in the area.[17] Many fires and decades later, twenty-seven horses burned to death in a tragic fire in a three-story stable in the alley extending west from Hanover Place between O, N, North Capitol, and First Streets NW.[18] The stable was filled with horses that pulled street-cleaning equipment. As recounted by the local press, the night watchman was outside watering a horse when one of the one hundred and three horses in the stable kicked over a lantern that set the building aflame within seconds. Firemen who responded to the fire alarm, stable workers, and local residents fought in vain to save the horses, many of which, terrified, would not budge from their stalls as flames flew up around them.[19]

In 1928, more than a decade after the last stable was built and almost thirty years after the first garage was constructed in the city, only one livery and boarding stable remained in operation. Four years later, it, too, would cease operation.

From Stables to Garages

As private car ownership developed in the 1910s and 1920s, so, too, did the need to store and service the vehicles. At first, new car owners simply remodeled existing stables and even alley dwellings to house their vehicles. Eventually, however, the garage as a building type was born, and today private garages to house cars dominate the city's alleys. Still, the transition from stable to garage was a gradual one, with the construction of the two different building types overlapping for almost twenty years from 1900 to 1919, when the first garage and the last stable were constructed in the city.[20]

The word "garage" did not make it into the English language until 1902. Until then, the garages were referred to as "auto barns" or "auto houses." As this transition was taking place, the early garage often served the dual purpose of housing horse and vehicle, much like that built by Edmund K. Fox in the alley behind his Georgetown house at 1618 Twenty-Ninth Street NW. The long, two-story, buff brick auto barn offered facilities for both horses and cars.

Four years earlier, the city's first known private garage, identified as an "auto house" on the building permit, was constructed at the rear of the French chateau–like house at 2201 Massachusetts NW. The garage, with its steeply pitched roof and rounded corner turrets, appears as a diminutive form of the much bigger and regal house it serves. From 1987 until 2009, Olga Hirshhorn, widow of art collector and philanthropist Joseph Hirshhorn, whose modern art and sculpture collection formed the foundation of the Smithsonian Institution's Hirshhorn Museum and Sculpture Garden, used the garage to house pieces of her own modern art collection.

During the 1910s chauffeurs' quarters were often included within garages, resulting in one-and-a-half- or

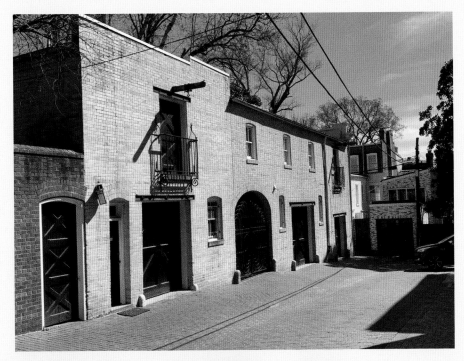

Early car garages were transitional buildings and often served the dual purpose of housing horse and vehicle. This one, described as an "auto barn" at the time of its construction in 1904, was built by banker and real estate business owner Edmund K. Fox in the alley at the rear of his Georgetown house at 1618 Twenty-Ninth Street NW. (Photo by author, 2021.)

Identified as an "auto house" on its 1900 building permit, this diminutive building at the rear of 2201 Massachusetts Avenue NW is the oldest known garage in the city. (Photo by Richard Williams, 2014.)

Garage rows, like this one in an alley between Flagler Place, First, U, and V Streets NW in Bloomingdale, were commonly built by developers behind blocks of rowhouses or apartment buildings. This row was constructed in the 1910s, along with several other similar rows at the center of the square. (Photo by author, 2014.)

two-story building forms that allowed for living quarters over the garage bay. But by the 1920s the garage had settled into its one-story, single-bay structure with a flat roof and no living quarters above. Individual car owners generally built their own independent garages at the rear of their house lots, but in other instances speculative builders constructed long and orderly rows of garages in the center of the squares in the city's expanding residential neighborhoods.

As new building types such as the garage emerged to accommodate new needs, obsolete building types such as stables found creative new uses and, with them, an entirely new alley demographic.

CHAPTER 6 Washington's Bohemia

DURING THE LATE nineteenth century, in a burgeoning city where building construction was a primary industry, architects, building contractors, craftspersons, and artists found affordable space in the city's alleys for their studios and workspaces. For decades these workshops and studios coexisted with alley residences, commercial and industrial enterprises, stables, and other utilitarian buildings. But as the horse-drawn era came to an end and former stables were left vacant and obsolete, those alley stables that had not already been converted to garages were ripe for new uses. By the 1920s artists, playwrights, restaurateurs, and other creatives seeking affordable space adapted the former stables to studios, theatrical spaces, teahouses, and nightclubs, establishing active yet tranquil communities away from the increasingly congested and noisy automobile-filled streets. Newspaper reporters who covered the city's artistic community toured the alleys and the artists' studios, dubbing several Washington's "Latin Quarter" or "Greenwich Village."

Alley Studios

Studios like that of sculptor Henry Jackson Ellicott, built in 1894 in the alley at the rear of Ellicott's residence at 1752 S Street NW in Dupont Circle, captured the imagination of the local press:

> In the studio there is every environment to make the lover of Bohemianism linger around. It is in the heart of the square bounded by Riggs, R, Seventeenth and Eighteenth streets northwest. If you enter from the alley, the true Bohemian approach, you come to a barn-like gable-roofed structure. It is like nothing else in the city. Through a little door you go into a huge, high-walled room, windowless, but with floods of light pouring through a glass roof. Then you are surrounded with a very atmosphere of statues, finished, half-finished and mutilated, with accompaniments of half-filled barrels of clay and plaster. Dust-covered busts abound, perched on boxes of sculptor's tools, and scaffold. And lots of other paraphernalia, all sculpturesque, and all of which to make the scene picturesque.[1]

Henry Ellicott was a direct descendent of Andrew Ellicott, the surveyor who in the late eighteenth

During the early twentieth century, artists and craftspersons moved into several of the city's alleys, converting abandoned stables, garages, and warehouses into affordable studio spaces. One such alley, Hillyer Court in Dupont Circle, was home to the Studio Group, whose shared studio space occupied a row of former alley dwellings. The University of Maryland Center for Art and Knowledge at the Phillips Collection is housed in two of the surviving buildings, continuing the tradition of the cultivation of art in the city's alleys. (Photo by author, 2021.)

Sculptor Henry Ellicott built this studio at the rear of his residence at 1752 S Street NW in 1894. The building remained an artist's studio for decades after his death in 1901. (Photo by Katie Williams, 2021.)

century was responsible for delineating the land that would become the District of Columbia and would later complete the Plan of the City of Washington, designed by Pierre L'Enfant.[2] Almost a century later and with a natural talent for drawing, Henry Ellicott attended the Academy of Design in New York City, where he studied under Emanuel Leutze, famous for his paintings *Washington Crossing the Delaware* (1851), at the Metropolitan Museum of Art in New York, and *Westward Ho* (1862), which hangs in the US Capitol. Ellicott also worked under and was inspired by sculptor and muralist Constantino Brumidi, whose works include the fresco *Apotheosis of Washington* (1865), located in the rotunda of the Capitol. After completing his studies, Ellicott launched his career in New York but in 1885 moved to DC, where he joined a growing number of nationally recognized resident artists.[3]

Ten years after moving to Washington, Ellicott won an important commission to design and sculpt an equestrian statue of Gen. Winfield Scott Hancock, a prominent Union general of the Civil War and a former Democratic presidential candidate. To accomplish the task, Ellicott built his vast new studio with a steep gable roof and double-height interior space to accommodate the full height of the statue's plaster cast. Upon completion in 1895, the Hancock statue was mounted on its pedestal on the north side of Pennsylvania Avenue at Seventh Street NW, where it still stands today.

Ellicott's studio remained one for decades following his death in 1901.[4] The building continues to command its alley site, imbuing it still with a certain artistic charm. The Hancock equestrian is Ellicott's only known work in Washington, but others can be found in public spaces up and down the East Coast, including two monuments at Gettysburg, an equestrian statue to Gen. George B. McClelland in Philadelphia, and many others in Pennsylvania, New York, Massachusetts, and North Carolina.

John Joseph Earley and Daly Court

Other sculptors, architects, craftspersons, and artisans established their own studios and workshops in the city's alleys. Some of these were temporary, like that of Paul Bartlett, who came to DC to work on the sculptural relief for the pediments capping the House and Senate wings of the US Capitol. Other artists, including John Joseph Earley, George Julian Zolnay, and Cleon Throckmorton, were more permanent residents and important fixtures in Washington's art scene. Their alley studios, art classes, exhibits, and other events enticed other artists into the alleys, creating several enclaves of artistic alley communities.

John Joseph Earley was a sixth-generation sculptor and native Washingtonian who had a profound impact on building in DC and beyond. Earley apprenticed with his sculptor father, James Earley, who had immigrated to the United States as a young man and established a stone-carving business in DC around 1892. Upon his father's death in 1906, John Earley inherited the business, built a sales office at 2131 G Street NW in Foggy Bottom and a studio at the rear. The studio, up against Daly Court, is, like the Ellicott Studio, a lofty, two-story brick structure capped by a tall gable roof with an expansive skylight that allowed

for an abundance of light in the open workspace. Within five years, Earley was joined by French-born sculptor Marie Bussard, who set up her own studio in the court immediately adjacent to Earley's. With her sculptor husband, August Bussard, Marie immediately began carving the intricate stonework for their French Tudor–style house at 2129 G Street NW. For more than a quarter of a century, Daly Court—now a pedestrian path known as Bausell Walk behind the Gelman Library on the George Washington University campus—was alive with the activity of artisans and craftsmen.

Here Earley and his team began to experiment with what became known as architectural concrete. At the time, poured concrete and precast concrete were strictly limited to structural uses, to be covered with stucco or paint, and were not used as a finish material. But Earley introduced and wisely patented the "Earley Process," a method of exposing the aggregate in concrete to create an unusual, pebbly aesthetic finish that would define his career.[5] Earley's first extensive use of the practice in DC was undertaken on the walls, balustrades, stairs, and other structural features of Meridian Hill Park in Northwest (today also called Malcolm X Park). The Earley Process continued to evolve over time and is readily recognizable, particularly for its extensive and ornamental use of color embedded in the concrete. Mosaic-like surfaces of Earley concrete are found citywide above the entrance to the bird and reptile houses at the National Zoo, in the ceilings of the Department of Justice Building's entry hall, and in the interior of the Shrine of the Sacred Heart.

Sculptor Paul Wayland Bartlett set up a temporary studio on Randolph Place NE in Washington's Eckington neighborhood, east of North Capitol Street and north of Florida Avenue, while working on the sculptural relief for the US Capitol. This 1916 photo shows the sculptor in his studio at work on a plaster model for the *Apotheosis of Democracy*, which fills the east portico of the House of Representatives wing of the Capitol. (Library of Congress.)

Washington sculptors John J. Earley and George Julian Zolnay collaborated on the 1921 rebuilding of Nashville's Parthenon. Zolnay provided the clay models for the architectural details of the entablature, while Earley finished the building using his distinctive architectural concrete, imbued with color, a trademark of the "Early Process." (Photo by Halsey Howard, 2021.)

One of Earley's most notable commissions, however, is found outside of DC in Tennessee. In 1921, when the city of Nashville—the "Athens of the South"—decided to rebuild its temporary replica of the Parthenon, which had been erected twenty-four years earlier as part of the centennial celebration of the state of Tennessee, city officials commissioned Earley to produce the building's architectural concrete finish. This included the bright red background of the metopes and tympanum and the blue of the mutules of the building's pediment, colors selected based on a scholarly assessment of the accurate coloration of the Athenian temple's ornamentation.[6] Earley worked with fellow Washington artist and sculptor George Julian Zolnay, who had sculpted the plaster pediment figures of the 1896 temple. Zolnay made clay models of the metopes and triglyphs for the new temple that were then cast in concrete in Earley's studio.

In 1936, after being denied permission to build a stone-crushing plant on the site, John Earley moved his business to larger quarters in suburban Virginia. He died in 1945, but the studio continued operating until 1954, when the Marietta Concrete Corporation purchased the company and its patented process.[7]

The Krazy Kat Klub

While many members of Washington's artistic community erected purpose-built studios in the city's alleys, others moved into abandoned stables and garages. Several alleys, from Green's Court downtown to St. Matthew's and Hillyer Courts in Dupont Circle to the so-called Artists' Alley in Georgetown, became veritable artist colonies. Local artists seeking affordable space and a shared community discovered the spacious former stables and relatively tranquil setting of the city's alleys. In 1922, having explored New York's Greenwich Village, *Washington Post* reporter Victor Flambeau "set out on a quest" to seek a "Quartier Latin" in Washington—some hidden haunt and center of the arts where the art-inspired have "renounced the commercial world with its seductive wealth, to gain in solitude or blithe companionship another kind of wealth and fame in self-expression."[8]

Flambeau found that place in Green's Court, immediately south of Thomas Circle, where artist Cleon Throckmorton—a former prize-winning art student from DC's McKinley Technical High School—opened a Bohemian café/speakeasy called the Krazy Kat Club in 1919. Throckmorton, whom reporter Victor Flambeau described as "some lost pre-Raphaelite, fallen by mistake into the Capital," established the club to support his painting career.[9] Occupying a former garage or stable, the club—"as weird and crazy as its name"—was furnished with rustic handmade furniture, lit with candles, warmed by a blazing open fire, and featured a well-used dance floor and theatrical space. Its real draw, however, was the garden courtyard and treehouse—a "spreading tree with airy rookeries built in its branches"— reached by a twelve-rung ladder. Waiters ferried drinks up the ladder to club-goers seated at the treehouse's only table.

Throckmorton, whose reputation as an artist was gaining ground in the city's art circles such as the Arts Club of Washington, ran the café with the help of his model-*cum*-wife, Katherine "Kat" Mullen, herself a sketch artist.[10] The Krazy Kat Klub, or the Kat, or Throck's, as it alternately came to be called, was intended as a club for artists, musicians, playwrights, and intellectuals.[11] A sketch of the Krazy Kat Klub by Mullen appeared in a 1921 *Washington Herald* news article highlighting the city's artistic scene. Its caption notes that the club was the city's "Bohemian stronghold," where the "disciples of the modern gather over the coffee cups to exercise the iconoclastic and creative spirits."[12] But the Krazy Kat quickly attracted a raucous crowd not necessarily there for artistic expression. After several police raids in 1919 in which patrons were arrested for disorderly conduct, the club closed temporarily. When it reopened in early 1920,

During Prohibition, Cleon Throckmorton's Krazy Kat Klub catered to artists, musicians, playwrights, and intellectuals. The brick stable building at right in this 1921 photo still survives and is home to a nightclub. (Library of Congress.)

The Krazy Kat Klub's main draw was its garden courtyard and treehouse, complete with table and chairs and bar service. In this 1921 photograph, Throckmorton (center) is sitting at the table with others. (Library of Congress.)

Throckmorton emphasized that the Krazy Kat was for "people interested in 'creative work'" and further wrote in a letter to the *Washington Herald*,

> The management is very sorry for the various things that are whispered about and said to occur in Washington's last clutch on Bohemia. Though this reputation would be worth a small fortune in New York, it nevertheless keeps many people away here, so if you will try to explain to your timid friends that because artists gather in a little place in an alley it does not necessarily make this place a den of vice and iniquity just because all artists are said to be devilishly inclined.[13]

Either in jest or in earnest, a new sign at the club's entrance read, "The Use of Intoxicating Beverages Is Absolutely Forbidden." After its reopening and for the next ten years, the Kat thrived. It was the scene of live theatrical performances—at least two of which had been written there—and hot jazz concerts. In July 1921 Throckmorton declared that the alley venue "proved, not only a club for artists, but a source of supply for musicians and playwrights."[14]

This row of private stables was built in the late 1870s along the diagonal alley, later named St. Matthew's Court, at the rear of the 1700 block of N Street NW. Beginning in 1918 and throughout the next several decades, members of the city's artistic community repurposed the stables as studios, a café and restaurant, and a popular theater. (Photo by author, 2021.)

St. Matthew's Court

The Krazy Kat Klub was a fixture in Washington's artistic community for most of the 1920s. But in 1928 the club closed when "Throck" left DC for New York to become a full-time set designer for Broadway plays. The Krazy Kat was not the city's only such venue, however. When asked by a reporter in 1921 where the city's artistic Bohemia might be, Dr. Mitchell Carroll, vice president of the Arts Club of Washington, secretary of the Archaeological Society, and editor of *Art and Archaeology* magazine, unequivocally declared, "St. Matthew's Alley is a very superior Greenwich Village."[15] For the next many decades, a series of artists established studios in the attached former stables that still line the alley behind St. Matthew's Cathedral. "There," proclaimed Mitchell Carroll, "you will find the studios of Miss Ellen Day Hale, Miss Catharine Critcher, and Mr. Zolnay."[16]

The last-named artist, George Julian Zolnay, was a Romanian-born Washington sculptor of national fame credited with establishing the alley as an artists' community in 1918. In the shadow of the dome of St. Matthew's Cathedral, the eponymous alley runs diagonally through the trapezoidal-shaped square bounded by Connecticut Avenue on the west, Seventeenth Street on the east, Rhode Island Avenue on the south, and N Street on the north. In the late 1870s, before construction of St. Matthew's Cathedral, developers Hayward & Hutchinson built a series of brick townhouses along the south side of the 1700 block of N Street NW, with a row of stables at their rear. These and other stables, including one

built by Alexander Graham Bell (who had a laboratory nearby), were home to equines and their coachmen during the late nineteenth and early twentieth centuries.

Before Zolnay moved into St. Matthew's Court in 1918, it had already earned a reputation as the home of the elegant prancing bays stabled there for Gen. Nelson A. Miles. A colorful character who served in the Civil War, the American Indian Wars, and the Spanish-American War, Miles moved to DC in 1895 as the last commanding general of the United States Army before the office was abolished in 1903. Upon taking up his post, Miles lived first at Twentieth and G Streets NW but soon purchased a house at 1734 N Street NW along with the stable at its rear. Like the other stables along St. Matthew's Court, his was built of red brick. But General Miles renovated and added on to the utilitarian building, fashioning it into a stucco-clad Spanish Mission–style building inspired by the architecture of the American Southwest, where he had spent much of his military career.

During Miles's residency in the city, his home was "one of the most noted of capital homes," and General Miles and his bays were apparently a familiar sight "to old and young" around town.[17] When General Miles retired and left the city for European travels in 1908, he sold his stable of horses, save one—Duke—which he gave to vaudevillian Buffalo Bill, who apparently used him as a lead horse in his shows.[18] More than a decade later, in 1922, the General Federation of Women's Clubs bought Miles's former N Street home for its headquarters, along with the rear court stable. Like the area artists who adapted the former

Interior court of a former stable owned by Gen. Nelson A. Miles in 1905. The building is now part of Iron Gate Restaurant. (Photo by author, 2012.)

stables into studios, the federation converted its stable building, first into a tearoom and two years later into a restaurant for fine dining.

The club renovated the interior to accommodate a state-of-the-art kitchen but otherwise retained many of its historical features. The horse stalls, creatively repurposed as dining booths, were each identified by name plates inscribed with the names of the horses once boarded there.[19] The upper-level hayloft, reached by a boxed stair, was reserved for private parties and pronounced by the press as a "good place for philosophers."[20] By 1928 and ever since, with a short hiatus, a restaurant known as Iron Gate has occupied the former stables as well as an outdoor patio sheltered by a gigantic vine of wisteria creating coveted summer shade.

Around the same time that the General Federation of Women's Clubs opened its teahouse, Zolnay and several other artists were well on their way to transforming St. Matthew's Court into an artists' community. A journalist reporting on the phenomenon noted that the court had been lifted from "obscure rear roadway" to a "MacDougal Alley" in "an almost exact reproduction of Greenwich Village's rendezvous for artists."[21]

The alley's transition from stables to studios began in 1918 when George Zolnay's workshop at Fifteenth and E Streets NW was commandeered by the government for war purposes. Although he intended the move to be only temporary, Zolnay remained in the alley, attracting other artists, with whom he established a permanent artists' enclave that would last into the 1960s. Zolnay and his family lived at

In 1922, the General Federation of Women's Clubs converted General Miles's stable building at the rear of 1734 N Street NW into a tearoom and shortly thereafter into a restaurant, known today as Iron Gate. The restaurant is shown here in a circa 1922 photograph. (Library of Congress.)

WASHINGTON, D. C.
CARNAHAN PRESS, Series No. 1

SCULPTOR ZOLNAY'S STUDIO
AT FIFTEENTH AND E STREETS

In 1923 well-known sculptor George Julian Zolnay established his artist studio in a former stable in St. Matthew's Court in Dupont Circle, where he inspired other artists to do the same. For ten years before moving into the alley, Zolnay had his studio at Fifteenth and E Streets NW, across from the grounds of the White House. (Collection of John DeFerrari.)

1738 N Street NW in front of his studio. Between his home and studio, he and his family created a garden where he would host fellow artists during the summer months.[22]

When Zolnay moved into the alley, he was already an accomplished and well-established artist. He had come to the United States in an official capacity to attend the World's Columbian Exposition in Chicago in 1893, and after traveling around and becoming enamored of the country, he decided to stay. Zolnay's career was launched two years later when he won the commission to design a plaster replica of the marble statuary in the pediment of the Greek Parthenon in Athens for the Parthenon in Nashville, mentioned above. That commission garnered him others, including many statues of former Confederate leaders.[23]

Although he was dubbed the "Sculptor of the Confederacy" for his Confederate statues, Zolnay's talent extended beyond such statuary. In DC Zolnay also sculpted the frieze at Central (later Cardozo) High School (1916) and the statue of Sequoyah (1917) that stands in the US Capitol's Statuary Hall.

Zolnay was soon joined in St. Matthews's Court by Ellen Day Hale, a portrait and mural painter; Gabriella P. Clements, also a muralist, who shared studio space with Hale; and Catherine Critcher, a successful portrait and figure painter. After establishing her studio there, Critcher opened, in 1923, the Critcher School of Painting and Commercial Art nearby at 1726 Connecticut Avenue. Critcher and Zolnay were both practicing artists and teachers, active in the Washington Arts Club. In fact, a portrait

Artist George Julian Zolnay posing with a model in his St. Matthew's Court NW studio in 1923. The model is for a memorial to fallen World War I soldiers located at the edge of Centennial Park in Nashville, Tennessee. (Library of Congress.)

that Critcher painted of Zolnay hung on the wall of her St. Matthew's Court studio.[24] Zolnay apparently held daily classes outside in the alley, bringing further attention to it. As reported by the *Washington Times* in 1921, Zolnay's students were "scholars . . . [and] children of the rich and many persons famous socially in the capital."[25] At the same time, Critcher opened her studio to a group of actors who practiced in the alley, perhaps inspiring the rise of a theater (called the Theater Lobby) there two decades later.

Over the next few decades, these artists overlapped with and were succeeded by others. When *Washington Post* reporter Virginia Lee Warren explored the alley in 1934, she proclaimed that "the little court, a labyrinth of studios . . . is Washington's Bohemia. . . . Here live painters and sculptors. In these studios, which were formerly stables, actually dwell artists, those gay devils supposed to have a peculiar genius for loose living and hell-raising in general. But while New York's Greenwich Village has free love and Paris'

During his tenure at the Treasury Department's Section of Fine Arts from 1934 to 1943, artist Edward Rowan pursued his own art, keeping a studio in St. Matthew's Court NW, pictured here. (Photograph by Lewis P. Woltz, Smithsonian Institution, Archives of American Art, Edward Beatty Rowan Papers.)

Latin Quarter has bacchanalian orgies, the Capital's Bohemia has only decorum, peace and a certain quaint, full-flavored beauty."[26]

The reporter's explorations led her into the studio of Critcher, up a narrow, steep flight of stairs and into "an enormous, white-walled room with a skylight letting in the precious north light. . . . The whole thing was as neat as a New England parsonage. But there was nothing prim or austere about the pictures arranged in orderly fashion around the big, clean room. Those glowing canvases seemed to pulse with life and beauty," Warren opined.[27]

While still a fixture in the alley during the 1930s, Catherine Critcher was joined by other artists, including Brian Brown, a caricaturist whose commercial work included wall decorations for nightclubs and barrooms; mural painter Dan Rhodes; portrait painter Bjorn Egeli; and painter, sculptor, and teacher Edward Beatty Rowan who from 1934 to 1943 was in DC as the assistant director to the Treasury Department's Section of Fine Arts, a New Deal program that oversaw the creation of public art in federal buildings.[28]

During the 1950s St. Matthew's Court was still home to Iron Gate Restaurant and was the newly established quarters for the Theater Lobby, which reopened in 1956 in its "intimate playhouse" in the court. The theater, sited at the intersection of the access alley from Rhode Island Avenue and the court, was a popular theatrical venue into the 1960s, attracting members of the city's political and social elite. As the theater rolled out the red carpet for Washington society and its diplomatic and political officials, only one artist—sculptor Bruce Moore—still kept a studio in the court. In 1957 Moore, who was then sculpting a larger-than-life bronze statue of military aviation pioneer Billy Mitchell for the Smithsonian Museum, lamented the change in scene as rents in the court had gone sky-high. A higher-income demographic was moving in and pricing the artists out.[29]

Hillyer Court and Artists' Alley

At least two other DC alleys developed as sizable artist communities before and after World War II: Hillyer Court NW in Dupont Circle, behind the Phillips Gallery, and Artists' Alley, in a row of alley stables in Georgetown. A group of artists that called themselves the Studio Group but were alternately known as the Hillyer Court group established their collective studio in Hillyer Court, now the University of Maryland Center for Art and Knowledge at the Phillips Collection (see page 94). They were primarily sculptors fully immersed in their artistic expression, from materials to product. Rather than buy supplies at art stores, they would dig their own clay, make tools of stone and wood, and develop colors by grinding rocks.[30] Ceramacist Katherine Hobbs, the leader of the group, built a reputation for her miniature clay animal sculptures painted in fanciful colors. The artists were all active in the Washington arts scene and held exhibitions at their Hillyer Court studio for years in the late 1940s and early 1950s.[31]

In 1953 Hobbs spearheaded the Artists' Mart in Georgetown—a gallery dedicated to exhibiting the

Artists' Alley, in the 3300 block between O and P Streets NW in Georgetown. The former stables-*cum*–artists' studios remain in residential use. (Photo by author, 2021.)

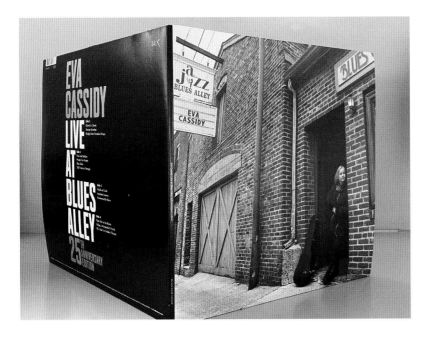

In 1965 the Blues Alley jazz nightclub opened its doors in a renovated shell of a nineteenth-century stable in Georgetown. Twenty years later, the original owners credited the club's dimly lit interiors, exposed brick walls, and "seedy elegance" for its appeal to musicians and patrons alike. In 1996 musician Eva Cassidy recorded her album *Live at Blues Alley* there, and a photo of her in front of the venue, taken by Larry Melton, became the album's cover. (Photo of album by author, 2022.)

work of local artists—and soon moved her studio from Hillyer Court to a row of stables in an alley behind the 3300 block of O and P Streets in Georgetown. Hobbs and three other women artists with whom she shared studio space dubbed the place "Artists' Alley."

By 1960 the renovation of Georgetown's historic buildings, including its alleys, was already well underway.[32] Today a new generation of residents, artists, restaurateurs, and entrepreneurs of all sorts are finding inspiration in DC's historic alleys.

CHAPTER 7   Reimagining Alleys

IN 1978, in response to the demolition of the alleys of the city of St. Louis, author Grady Clay wrote, "Out of sight and out of mind, the American residential alley has been the academic, geographic and social outcast of the built environment. . . . It is now time to consider what the alley is, and what it might become—a hidden resource waiting to be recognized."[1] Increasingly in more recent years, urban planners and architects nationwide are agreeing with this sentiment. As Philadelphia-based architect Thomas Dougherty points out in *The American Alley: A Hidden Resource*, American cities are automobile-centric, and the alleys, with their narrow widths and informal and intimate-scaled buildings, are the few places that allow for the development of pedestrian-scaled urban spaces.[2] Similarly, landscape architect and social historian Michael David Martin found that alleys provide "spatial enclosure" that allows for greater social activity and engagement than in other urban settings. As such, alleys can become "containers for the magic of city life."[3]

To encourage socially active and intimate urban spaces and to provide additional housing in increasingly populous cities, city and county governments are developing building codes and ordinances to encourage the development of underutilized alleys. Andrés Duany, founder of the Congress for the New Urbanism, was an early proponent of reintroducing alleys into building codes, which he did in his traditional town plans for Seaside, Florida, and Kentlands, Maryland, in the 1990s. Since then, many cities have passed legislation that allows for the introduction and redevelopment of alleys.

In Washington, DC, the appeal of alleys as intimate spaces was rediscovered decades before this more recent revival. When a Whiter and wealthier demographic moved into the long-inhabited alleys of Georgetown, Foggy Bottom, and Capitol Hill in the late 1940s and 1950s, they provided necessary upgrades and renovations and successfully overturned a congressional mandate to eradicate them. But this preservation movement was limited to inhabited alleys in certain residential neighborhoods. Other alleys, no longer occupied with residences or businesses, became neglected spaces, with abandoned buildings and open lots given over to warehousing, storage, and parking.

The enclosed space, intimate scale, and informal nature of this group of historic stable buildings in a Capitol Hill alley provide just the conditions that urban planners claim encourage a sense of shared public space and social gathering. (DC Historic Preservation Office, 2014.)

Approximately one hundred years after its construction in 1907, this former stable at 1835 (Rear) Fifth Street NW in LeDroit Park was renovated into a private residence and artist studio. (DC Historic Preservation Office, 2014.)

In recent years, as urban planners recognized that the city's historic alleys offered opportunities for greater density and the potential for more affordable housing options, the city revised and relaxed its zoning codes. Previously it was extremely difficult to convert non-residential buildings to residential uses in alleys, but now any existing alley building can be adapted for residential purposes, and new dwellings can also be built on alley lots. Furthermore, accessory dwelling units can be built on the same lot of a principal dwelling at its rear and along the alleys.

These changes in DC's zoning regulations came about in response to urban planning and real estate development pressures—population growth, soaring real estate prices, and a shortage of housing—that have been building for years. As in the nineteenth century, individuals looking for cheaper housing options looked to the city's abandoned and underused alleys. In 2006, as photographer Steven Cummings sought affordable quarters in a city of increasingly high real estate costs, he moved his photography studio into a former stable in an alley off H and Eighth Streets NE, informing a *Washington Post* reporter, "Alleys are the place to go." Around the same time, filmmaker Kyle Kreutzberg also took to the alleys and established his studio in a former stable in LeDroit Park. There

This stable, constructed in 1892 to service the house at 1621 Connecticut Avenue NW in Dupont Circle, was renovated and converted into a Pilates studio in the past decade. (DC Historic Preservation Office, 2014.)

Kreutzberg cleared the lot of overflowing garbage, renovated the brick stable, landscaped a patio with lush greenery, and created a minioasis within the protected confines of the surrounding building fabric.[4]

Today, however, the city's alleys rarely provide affordable housing options. For the past many decades, individuals, speculative builders, and developers have been buying up alley lots and alley buildings and introducing custom-designed alley dwellings and commercial operations such as restaurants, cafés, and yoga studios that cater to a high-income demographic.

For the most part, these new buildings are located in areas zoned for low density and/or are in one of the District's officially designated historic districts and are thus subject to historic preservation review. Consequently, even as their socioeconomic character is being turned upside down, the alleys and their buildings retain their historic low-scale and vernacular character.

In the Blagden Alley and Naylor Court Historic District, rows of alley dwellings, once home to the poorest of the city's residents, private stables, commercial liveries, and light-manufacturing concerns, have been renovated and retain their historical character. They now, however, boast residences that are no longer affordable to many, a boutique coffee shop,

Many of the historic alley buildings in Blagden Alley NW have been renovated and converted to new uses. In 2014 La Colombe Coffee Roasters renovated and moved into this 1909 stable building, which was standing vacant. (DC Historic Preservation Office, 2021.)

This pair of dwellings was built in the early 2000s in Brown's Court SE in the Capitol Hill Historic District. The contemporary alley dwellings are in keeping with the traditional nineteenth-century alley dwelling forms that define Brown's Court and other residential alleys. (DC Historic Preservation Office, 2014.)

high-end restaurants, design firms, art galleries, and the outdoor DC Alley Museum. Multitudes who in past decades would not venture into an alley now traverse this internal space freely, seeking shortcuts to the public streets, strolling past the murals that are part of the museum, or patronizing the eateries and other businesses there.

As Blagden Alley and Naylor Court have been undergoing their transformation in a piecemeal fashion, Cady's Alley in Georgetown was completely redeveloped in a wholesale manner. Named for Dennis T. Keady who operated a saloon at 3314 M Street NW in the late nineteenth century and who built the row of alley dwellings toward the alley's west end at

Thirty-Fourth Street, Cady's Alley (variously called "Katy's Court" and "Keady Court" has been fully transformed. The developer EastBanc renovated the rear elevations of several M Street–facing commercial buildings that extended to the alley, renovated abutting alley buildings, and introduced infill construction that extended the full block of the narrow lane above the C&O Canal. Once home to buildings and workers associated with the port town and its industries, Cady's Alley is now home to high-end design and apparel stores and restaurants.

Other sizable development projects have also incorporated alleys and alley buildings into new construction. Built in 2007, the Flats at Union Row, at

Located just above the C&O Canal, Cady's Alley historically served as the home for the businesses and workers associated with Georgetown's waterfront industry. Vacant and underutilized, the alley and its buildings were redeveloped in the early 2000s to accommodate premium home design and apparel retailers that took advantage of and added to the loft-like spaces of the former warehouse and stable buildings. Cady's Alley has been recognized by both the design and historic preservation communities for its successful rediscovery of a utilitarian urban space. (DC Historic Preservation Office, 2014.)

the corner of Fourteenth and V Streets NW, is a nine-story condominium project whose principal street-facing building spans the historic Chester Court (renamed Union Row). In the nineteenth century, Chester Court was lined with two-story brick alley dwellings, but beginning in 1913 they were demolished by the Elite Laundry Company for a series of industrial-scale concrete structures for its laundry plant. The new condominium complex incorporated these concrete-frame buildings into its plan, instilling the courtside buildings of Union Row with the industrial-like character of the former laundry facility and opening the court to pedestrian activity.

Another wholesale development, City Center, built on the former Washington Convention Center site downtown and bounded by Ninth, Tenth, H, and I Streets NW, reintroduced a long-lost alley—Palmer Alley—into the large city square. Historically H-shaped, Palmer Alley was previously filled on all sides with stables, alley dwellings, sheds, and shops.

Built in 2007, the Flats at Union Row on Fourteenth Street north of V Street NW consist of a nine-story building whose principal street-facing building spans the historic Chester Court. The condominium complex retains a series of industrial warehouses that served the Elite Laundry Company in the early twentieth century. (DC Historic Preservation Office, 2014.)

In Prather's Alley NW in the Mount Vernon Triangle neighborhood, where extensive redevelopment is underway, this former blacksmith shop and warehouse (see photo on page 81) were retained and incorporated into a new, multistory apartment building. (Photo by author, 2021.)

The new alley, which cuts through the square and is entirely contemporary in layout and design, nonetheless reintroduces the sought-after intimacy of scale and communal space of its historic counterparts.

The city's historic alleys, many of which have been completed or are under redevelopment with upscale retail venues and a gentrifying clientele and residential base, offer a historical and social paradox. Once home to the city's most needy residents, they are now home to its most privileged. New and larger buildings of shiny steel and glass stand juxtaposed to smaller historic ones of brick. Some residents may object to the new and larger buildings that risk eroding the small-scale and intimate-sized alley character. Others may bemoan the increased activity of people and delivery trucks that the commercial venues bring. Still others may be offended by the expropriation of space from poor to wealthy and from Black to White. But given the overall success of the redevelopment of certain alleys, others are sure to follow. For good or ill, the hidden alleys of Washington are hidden no more.

NOTES

Chapter 1: The Origins of DC's Alleys

1. Mary Ellen Hayward, *Baltimore's Alley Houses: Homes for Working People since the 1780s* (Baltimore: Johns Hopkins University Press, 2008), 15.

2. At first Elfreth's Alley was nothing more than a path that stretched from Front Street to Second Street. Named after blacksmith and land developer Jeremiah Elfreth, the alley was later lined with tiny rowhouses and small commercial concerns. Elfreth's Alley, with its eighteenth-century rowhouses lining its narrow edges, survives as one of the oldest and best-preserved alleys in the country. http://www .elfrethsalley.org/.

3. Sara A. Hage, "Alleys: Negotiating Identity in Traditional, Urban and New Urban Communities" (master's thesis, University of Massachusetts, 2008), 5–6, notes that by law the enslaved were required to live on the property of their owners so they could be "properly watched over." Hage surmises that the alleys clearly delineated the edge of the land on which the enslaved were required to live and served to control the enslaved population.

4. James Borchert, *Alley Life in Washington: Family, Community, Religion, and Folklife in the City, 1850–1970* (Urbana: University of Illinois Press, 1982), 230.

5. David Swinney, "Washington: A City of Beauty and a City of Slums; Summary of a Thesis—'Alley Dwellings and Housing Reform in the District of Columbia,'" Washington Housing Association, 1938.

6. Although large lots were the norm in the original city plan, some squares, such as 503, 545, and 623, had more numerous lots with smaller dimensions. The existence of these smaller lots suggests that early city planners may have intended certain squares to be specifically developed as worker housing or for the construction of more affordable housing. Conversation with David Maloney, DC Historic Preservation Office, 2020.

7. Alleys with *H*- and *I*-shaped configurations were the most common alley forms in the original city, but others, including *X*-shaped, diagonal, and straight-through alleys, were also platted and appear in the original "Record of Squares." See https:// dcraonline-rms.dcra.dc.gov/SurDocsPublic/faces /Level106BookTypes.jsp for digitized images of each of the platted city squares. See also the plats

of individual squares in E. F. M. Faehtz and F. W. Pratt, *Real Estate Directory of the City of Washington* (Washington, DC: Faehtz & Pratt, 1874).

8. Daniel D. Reiff, *Washington Architecture, 1791–1861: Problems in Development* (Washington, DC: US Commission of Fine Arts, 1971), 25.

9. K Street was essentially the northern edge of the city in the pre–Civil War era. African Americans tended to live north of the street and Whites to the south. South and west of the core, Blacks dominated part of the low-lying lands in Southwest and in Foggy Bottom and were well represented in Georgetown. Borchert, *Alley Life*, 5–6.

10. Before the Civil War, individual owners would subdivide their own lots to create separate alley lots for rental or sale. By the 1870s, nonresident builders and developers moved increasingly into the market of subdividing and building on alley lots as a real estate venture. Borchert, 29–34.

11. Ellen Beasley, *The Alleys and Back Buildings of Galveston: An Architectural and Social History* (Houston: Rice University Press, 1996), as noted in Rebecca Summer, "Comparing Mid-Century Historic Preservation and Urban Renewal through Washington, DC's Alley Dwellings," *Journal of Planning History* 21, no. 2 (2021): 3.

12. Borchert's research is based on a census showing the population of alleys and courts in the District of Columbia, found in *Report of Commissioners of the District of Columbia for the Year Ended 1897*, vol. 1 (Washington, DC: Government Printing Office, 1897), 199–212.

13. Based on an examination of the 1858 city directory, Borchert counted 348 heads of households with alley addresses in forty-nine separate alleys. Borchert, *Alley Life*, 19. See also James Borchert, "Alley Life in Washington: An Analysis of 600 Photographs," *Records of the Columbia Historical Society* 49 (1973–74): 245.

14. Edith Elmer Wood, *The Housing of the Unskilled Wage Earner: America's Next Problem* (New York: Macmillan, 1919), 46. To support the theory that the first alley dwellings were built to house the enslaved, historian Daniel D. Swinney notes in his dissertation that an elderly woman told him that her father was a member of the Society of Friends, which before and during the Civil War built a number of dwellings in the alleys to shelter persons escaping slavery. Swinney further concludes that even if alley dwellings were not built as quarters for the enslaved in the city's earliest years, the interior alleys with their stables and outbuildings "naturally became a daily gathering place of domestic servants, of which the greater number were slaves." See Daniel D. Swinney, "Alley Dwellings and Housing Reform in the District of Columbia" (PhD diss., University of Chicago, 1938), 16, 18n2.

15. Swinney, "Alley Dwellings," 71. Borchert, *Alley Life*, 27, also cites Swinney. Swinney identifies the Snow in question as C. H. Snow, a partner in the Washington publishing house Snow, Coyle & Company and publisher of the *Daily National Intelligencer* newspaper from 1864 to 1869. Snow Alley was listed in the city directories beginning in 1860, and the Fahetz and Pratt plat maps, 1873–74, show four frame dwellings and a greenhouse in the square owned by Snow, giving credence to the story. However, research conducted by the author does not confirm the story. City directories show that Snow lived in various locations downtown but not in Foggy Bottom.

16. Swinney, "Alley Dwellings," 17.

17. *Daily National Intelligencer*, July 25, 1865, as quoted in Bethany Mae Emenhiser, "Hidden Communities: Creating a Preservation Plan for Underutilized Alleyways as a Tool for Reactivation" (master's thesis, Savannah College of Art and Design, 2015), 29.

18. *Daily National Intelligencer*, March 22, 1866.

19. Kathleen M. Lesko, Valerie Babb, and Carroll R. Gibbs, *Black Georgetown Remembered: A History of Its Black Community from the Founding of "The Town of George" in 1751 to the Present Day* (Washington, DC: Georgetown University Press, 1991), 19.

20. Report to Congress, Senate Document No. 1276, 42ff, as quoted in Swinney, "Alley Dwellings," 19.

21. This information is gleaned from research on the minor streets of Washington compiled by David Maloney, DC Historic Preservation Office, and based on subdivision plats located at the Office of the Surveyor of the District of Columbia, accessible at https://dcraonline-rms.dcra.dc.gov/SurDocsPublic /faces/t1.jsp.

22. Borchert, *Alley Life*, 5–7.

23. Borchert, 42.

24. "Tiger Alley: A Resort in Southeast Washington That Is the Scene of Frequent Brawls," Daily Critic, September 20, 1890. As quoted in "Lost Capitol Hill: Tiger Alley," *The Hill Is Home* (blog), accessed February 17, 2021, https://thehillishome.com/2010/03 /lost-capitol-hill-tiger-alley.

25. George M. Kober, *The History and Development of the Housing Movement in the District of Columbia* (Washington, DC: Washington Sanitary Improvement Company, 1897), 7.

26. See Grace Vawter Bicknell, *The Inhabited Alleys of Washington, D.C.* (Washington, DC: Committee on Housing, Woman's Welfare Department, National Civic Federation, 1912), 5. Bicknell speculates that the Board of Health's condemnation program was likely discontinued due to "the influence of men whose money interests were at stake." The construction costs of alley dwellings were low, and rents were comparatively high, making alley dwelling construction profitable for the few who then could exercise political influence. See also Jesse Thomas Jones, *Directory of the Inhabited Alleys of Washington, D.C.* (Washington, DC: Housing Committee Monday Evening Club, 1912).

27. A Women's Anthropological Society survey of alley houses in 1896 found in its sampling of alley dwellings that thirty-three were constructed of brick and seventeen were wooden. The report notes that the prevalence of wooden alley dwellings—34 percent of the total—is a "constant menace in thickly settled residence and business districts." George M. Kober, *Report on the Housing of the Laboring Classes in the City of Washington, D.C.* (Washington, DC: Government Printing Office, 1900), 109.

28. Borchert, *Alley Life*, 13–14.

29. Edith Elmer Wood, "Four Washington Alleys: Some Phases of Life in Fenton Place, Madison Alley, Essex Court and Naylor's Court as Brought Out in a Recent Survey," *The Survey* 31 (December 6, 1913): 250–52.

30. Constance McLaughlin Green in *Washington: Capital City, 1879–1950* (Princeton, NJ: Princeton University Press, 1963), 162, noted that in 1913 the US Senate requested a tabulation of alley dwellings. The results of the data collection identified more than one thousand different owners of alley dwellings citywide.

31. Kim Hoagland, "Nineteenth-Century Building Regulations in Washington, D.C.," *Records of the Columbia Historical Society* 52 (1989): 58.

32. Borchert, *Alley Life*, 22.

33. Report by the Committee of the District of Columbia on Senate Bill 101, Discontinuance of the Use as Dwellings of Buildings in the District of Columbia, March 1933, DC History Center.

34. Borchert, "Alley Life in Washington," 245.

Chapter 2: Alley Life

1. Message to Congress, December 1, 1904, as quoted in Swinney, "Alley Dwellings," 33; and Tom Lewis, *Washington: A History of Our National City* (New York: Basic Books, 2015), 335.

2. The term "alleyites" was frequently used in newspaper accounts of the late nineteenth and early twentieth centuries to describe residents of the city's inhabited alleys.

3. In a 1901 lecture titled "Southern Workman," Dr. W. E. B. Du Bois compared the congested alleys of the southern cities to the tenement slums of northern ones. Du Bois agreed with White reformers that alleys were not suited for housing people and that alley housing constituted "the most crushing indictment of the modern landlord system." "Alley Problem in the South," *Colored American*, December 14, 1901.

4. See "Helping the Poor: An Alley Workers' Conference," *Washington Bee*, March 19, 1910; and "Dr. Waldron's Great Work," *Washington Bee*, January 6, 1912.

5. Swinney, "Alley Dwellings," 137.

6. Godfrey Frankel and Laura Goldstein, *In the Alleys: Kids in the Shadow of the Capitol* (Washington, DC: Smithsonian Institution Press, 1995), 4, 9.

7. James Borchert, "Alley Landscapes of Washington," *Landscape* 23, no. 3 (1979): 286.

8. Mary Cromwell, "The Human Side of a 'Washington Alley'" (unpublished report for the Associated Charities of Washington, D.C., May 1915), 6.

9. Kober, *Report on the Housing*, 110.

10. Wood, "Four Washington Alleys," 251; Swinney, "Alley Dwellings," 41.

11. In her survey, Edith Elmer Wood noted that the shopkeeper rented the rooms on a weekly basis and at the time of her survey all the rooms were taken. Wood, "Four Washington Alleys," 251.

12. Ben Bradlee, "Life in an Alley within Shadow of Capitol Dome," *Washington Post*, December 19, 1948.

13. Cromwell, "Human Side," 5.

14. Borchert, *Alley Life*, 168.

15. Cromwell, "Human Side," 6.

16. Cromwell, 6.

17. Cromwell, 6.

18. Cromwell, 6.

19. Wood, "Four Washington Alleys," 250.

20. Borchert, *Alley Life*, 145–47.

21. As quoted in Frankel and Goldstein, *In the Alleys*, 38.

22. As quoted in Frankel and Goldstein, 35.

23. *Washington Star*, December 27, 1881, as quoted in Borchert, *Alley Life*, 131.

Chapter 3: Humanitarian Reform Efforts

1. Hayward, *Baltimore's Alley Houses*, 218.

2. Hayward, 225.

3. Lewis, *Washington*, 238.

4. Charles F. Weller, *Neglected Neighbors: Stories of Life in the Alleys, Tenements and Shanties of the National Capital* (Philadelphia: John C. Winston, 1909), 10.

Willow Tree Alley in Southwest was located on the present-day site of the Wilbur Cohen Social Security Administration Building, on the south side of Independence Avenue SW.

5. Swinney, "Alley Dwellings," 27.

6. Mary Clare de Graffenried, "Typical Alley Houses in Washington, D.C.," *Women's Anthropological Society Bulletin*, no. 7 (1897). See also Borchert, "Alley Life in Washington," 244–59. The published report was based on an extensive study of thirteen of the surveyed alleys, covering fifty alley dwellings, occupied by 248 persons. See William Henry Jones, *The Housing of Negroes in Washington, D.C.: A Study in Human Ecology* (Washington, DC: Howard University Press, 1929), 35.

7. Carolyn Swope, "The Problematic Role of Public Health in Washington, D.C.'s Urban Renewal," *Public Health Reports* 133, no. 6: 707; Borchert, *Alley Life*, 183.

8. Weller, *Neglected Neighbors*, 4.

9. Weller, 5.

10. National Register of Historic Places, "St. James Mutual Homes," Washington, DC, 2016, no. 1600027. See Paul A. Groves, "The Development of a Black Residential Community in Southwest Washington: 1860–1897," in *Records of the Columbia Historical Society, Washington, D.C.*, vol. 49, *1973–74* (Washington, DC: Columbia Historical Society, 1974).

11. Chris Meyers Asch and George Derek Musgrove, *Chocolate City: A History of Race and Democracy in the Nation's Capital* (Chapel Hill: University of North Carolina Press, 2017), 197–98.

12. "Mr. Riis Denounces Slums of the City: Alleys and Blind Streets of Capital City Characterized as Worse Than Whitechapel," *Washington Times*, December 16, 1903.

13. Asch and Musgrove, *Chocolate City*, 203.

14. "Views Squalid Shacks and the City's Slums," *Washington Times*, April 8, 1905; *Evening Star*, May 5, 1905.

15. *Evening Star*, January 30, 1903.

16. Asch and Musgrove, *Chocolate City*, 203.

17. "The Nation's Stately Capital Contains Slums Which for Immoral and Unsanitary Conditions Vie with Those of London and Constantinople," *New York Tribune*, May 3, 1903.

18. Wilbur Vincent Mallalieu, "A Washington Alley," *The Survey* 29 (October 19, 1912): 70.

19. Cromwell, "Human Side." Cromwell's unpublished report provides findings of her study of alley residents in one particular alley, which she refers to as "Alley K." Her research was based on fifty-five "family groups" who lived there.

20. Thomas Jesse Jones, "The Alley Homes of Washington," *The Survey* 29 (October 19, 1912): 68.

21. Swope, "Problematic Role," 707–14.

22. "Clear out the Alleys," *Washington Post*, December 17, 1896.

23. As quoted in Asch and Musgrove, *Chocolate City*, 202.

24. As quoted in Lewis, *Washington*, 335.

25. Swinney, "Alley Dwellings," 37.

26. Constance Green notes that the reorganization of the Associated Charities in 1896 contributed to a shift in attitude about "pauperism" and that there was a growing acceptance of the idea that "the environment is as important as inherited character in making good citizens and thus a good city." Green, *Washington*, 149.

27. Asch and Musgrove, *Chocolate City*, 204.

28. "Alley Work Theme, Improvement Association to Discuss Its Activities," *Evening Star*, May 12, 1912; "In the Alleys," *Washington Bee*, March 19, 1910; "Helping the Poor: An Alley Workers' Conference," *Washington*

Bee, March 19, 1910; "Dr. Waldron's Great Work," *Washington Bee*, January 6, 1912.

29. "Dr. Waldron's Great Work," *Washington Bee*, January 6, 1912.

30. "Helping the Poor."

31. Swinney, "Alley Dwellings," 35.

32. National Register of Historic Places, "St. James Mutual Homes," 8–19.

33. *Evening Star*, May 5, 1905.

34. See "Willow Tree Alley," *Evening Star*, May 5, 1905; "Willow Tree Alley Soon to Be a Park," *Evening Star*, January 16, 1914; and "Willow Tree Alley to Be Beauty Spot," *Evening Star*, April 4, 1914.

35. "Transformation of Willow Tree Alley Adds Beauty Spot to Nation's Capital," *Sunday Star*, November 15, 1914.

36. "Tribute to Memory of President's Wife," *Sunday Star*, September 27, 1914.

37. Beth Hannold, "The Influence of Sanitary Housing Can Not Be Over Estimated," in *Housing Washington*, ed. Richard Longstreth (Chicago: Center for American Places, Columbia College, 2010), 133–57.

38. Among these techniques was the tenant management system instituted in Britain by Octavia Hill (1838–1912), which employed female rent collectors who provided tenants with friendly domestic and hygienic advice with the dual goal of improving their lives and enlisting their cooperation in making rent payments in full and on time and maintaining their properties. See Hannold, "Influence of Sanitary Housing," 134; and National Register of Historic Places, "St. James Mutual Homes," 8–19.

39. National Register of Historic Places, "St. James Mutual Homes," 8–19.

40. Kober, *History and Development*.

41. Kober, *Report of the Housing*, 116.

42. Hannold, "Influence of Sanitary Housing," 140.

43. Hannold, "Influence of Sanitary Housing," 152.

44. "Moral Issue Seen in Alley Project: Proper Housing for Persons Removed by Clearance Held Necessary," *Evening Star*, December 16, 1934.

45. "Ihlder Asks Aid in Alley Drive," *Evening Star*, January 1, 1935.

46. "Two Slum Clearance Projects Being Pushed Ahead Here: Drab Navy Place Obliterated in Southeast; Houses Going Up in Suburban Forest," *Evening Star*, December 19, 1939. Without any consideration to how displaced residents felt about leaving their communities behind, the local press proclaimed the new housing to be "a colony of pleasant homes for slum dwellers in the midst of a beautiful suburban forest" east of the Anacostia River.

47. See the *Evening Star*, July 7, 1940. The ADA received criticism for its emphasis on building affordable housing over slum clearance. In "Building Managers Criticize Operations of the Alley Authority: Elimination of Slums Declared Lagging behind Construction," *Evening Star*, March 2, 1940, the article notes that the number of units razed is but 46 percent of the number of new ones being built.

48. "Building Managers Criticize Operations of Alley Authority: Elimination of Slums Declared Lagging behind Construction," *Evening Star*, March 2, 1940. This shift in the ADA's mission toward building new housing before eliminating existing alley dwellings ultimately contributed to the retention of alley dwellings and their subsequent renovation.

49. John Ihlder, "Program of Alley Dwelling Authority Is Geared to Washington's Future," *Sunday Star*, June 16, 1940.

50. Ihlder, "Program of Alley Dwelling Authority."

51. "Hopkins Place Commemorates Crusader for Slum Clearance," *Evening Star*, October 21, 1936; "Dedication Today in London Court: First Real Accomplishment in Slum-Clearance Drive in Washington," *Evening Star*, October 20, 1936. See also "Charlotte Everett Wise Hopkins," Church of the Epiphany, September 5, 2017, https://epiphanydc.org/2017/09/05/september-7-charlotte-everett-wise-hopkins-1935/.

52. *Report of the Alley Dwelling Authority for the District of Columbia for the Fiscal Years 1936–37* (Washington, DC: Government Printing Office, n.d.).

53. "Housing Project Open to Colored," *Evening Star*, December 24, 1937.

54. "Plan to Exclude Colored in Area Meets Protest: Lincoln Association Seeks Admission to St. Mary's Project," *Washington Post*, July 22, 1937.

55. Asch and Musgrove, *Chocolate City*, 255. See also "Plan to Exclude Colored."

56. "Statement of Facts in re: Administration of the Alley Dwelling Authority Law Enacted June 12, 1934, and Amendments Thereto, as Observed, Experienced and Endured by Colored Citizens within the Territory of the Lincoln Civic Association," December 31, 1939, DC History Center.

57. "District's Slum Program Begun in Navy Place," *Evening Star*, September 12, 1939.

Chapter 4: Twentieth-Century Alley Renovation

1. In 1943, with Executive Order No. 9344, President Franklin D. Roosevelt changed the name of the Alley Dwelling Authority to the DC Housing Authority to more accurately reflect its new mission of using public funds to build affordable housing.

2. "Citizens Committee on Race Relations, Inc.: First Annual Report," August 1944, in box 163-19, folder 2, Charles Hamilton Houston Papers, Moorland-Spingarn Research Center, Howard University, Washington, DC. As quoted in Asch and Musgrove, *Chocolate City*, 281n103.

3. "Alley Moving Day for 20,000 to Be Delayed," *Washington Post*, March 15, 1944.

4. Lesko, Babb, and Gibbs, *Black Georgetown Remembered*, 41.

5. See From Slave Ship to Harvard, http://fromslaveship.blogspot.com\, for maps identifying the residency of African Americans in Georgetown in 1855 and 1871, as gleaned from city directories. The data was mapped by James H. Johnston, author of *From Slave Ship to Harvard: Yarrow Mamout and the History of an African American Family* (New York: Fordham University Press, 2015), and posted to his above blog.

6. Sandra Fitzpatrick and Maria R. Goodwin, *The Guide to Black Georgetown: Places and Events of Historical and Cultural Significance in the Nation's Capital*, rev. ed. (New York: Hippocrene Books, 2001), 199.

7. Kathryn Schneider Smith explains in *Port Town to Urban Neighborhood: The Georgetown Waterfront of Washington, D.C., 1880–1920*, Center for Washington Area Studies, George Washington University (Dubuque, IA: Kendall/Hunt, 1989), 82.

8. Green, *Washington*, 400.

9. Lesko, Babb, and Gibbs, *Black Georgetown Remembered*, 82.

10. Lesko, Babb, and Gibbs, 93.

11. As quoted in Rebecca Summer, "The Urban Alley: A Hidden Landscape of Social Change in Washington, D.C." (PhD diss., University of Wisconsin, 2019), 52.

12. Summer, 54–55.

13. "Ten Georgetown Families Face Condemnation Ouster," *Evening Star*, February 12, 1950.

14. Lesko, Babb, and Gibbs, *Black Georgetown Remembered*, 87–88.

15. "Ten Georgetown Families Face Condemnation."

16. "Be It Ever So Humble," *Evening Star*, February 13, 1950.

17. "Condemned Slum in Georgetown Alley Goes High Hat as Pomander Walk," *Evening Star*, September 14, 1951. See also Summer, "Urban Alley," 56.

18. "Condemned Slum in Georgetown Alley."

19. "Condemned Slum in Georgetown Alley."

20. "Condemned Slum in Georgetown Alley."

21. During the first decades of the twentieth century, Cecil Alley was home to working-class White residents, while the adjacent Cherry Hill Alley was entirely Black-occupied. Lesko, Babb, and Gibbs, *Black Georgetown Remembered*, 82.

22. "Private Owners Reclaiming Neighborhood Once Known as Capitol Hill 'Slum,'" *Evening Star*, August 23, 1947.

23. "Private Funds Have Rehabilitated Snow's Court," *Evening Star*, May 4, 1955.

24. Isabelle Shelton, "Foggy Bottom Area Gets Face Lifting," *Evening Star*, November 8, 1953.

25. Shelton.

26. Shelton.

27. Summer, "Urban Alley," 53.

28. Robert J. Lewis, "Owners Who Reclaimed Blighted Area Seek Street Status for Neighborhood," *Evening Star*, October 29, 1949; "Slum Area Goes 'Moderne,'" Washington Post, July 14, 1955.

29. "Alley in Foggy Bottom Gets Old English Flavor," *Washington Post*, June 21, 1961.

30. "Slum Alley Goes 'Moderne.'"

31. "Group Fights City Threat to Close Up Alley Homes," *Washington Post*, September 16, 1953.

32. "Once Alley Always an Alley under Law?" *Evening Star*, September 25, 1953.

33. "Once Alley Always an Alley Under Law?"; "Witnesses Appeal to Save Alley Homes," *Evening Star*, September 28, 1953; "Not All Alleys Are Slums," *Evening Star*, February 7, 1954; "Reprieve for Alleys," *Washington Post*, February 3, 1954; "Alley Dwelling Renovation Gets Council Backing," *Evening Star*, April 17, 1954; "Senate Gets Bill Repealing Alley Statute," *Washington Post*, May 25, 1954.

34. "Witnesses Appeal to Save Alley Homes"; "Remodeled Alley Houses Put Commissioners on Spot," *Washington Daily News*, September 21, 1953.

35. "One Cherry Hill Friend Sent a Tree Instead," *Evening Star*, May 15, 1955; "Stubbed Our Toe?" *Evening Star*, May 20, 1955; "New Look, Paving, Spur Alley Dance," *Washington Post*, May 15, 1955.

36. A sales ad for the house at 3207 Scott Place NW noted, "Unique miniature bachelor house with patio, combining the charm of age with new-house conveniences, as compact as an apartment, this detached house offers peaceful privacy." *Washington Post*, January 31, 1954.

37. "Georgetown Groups Fight Subdivision," *Washington Post*, March 10, 1956.

38. "Alley Congestion," *Washington Post*, July 29, 1956.

39. "City Drafts Ban on Some Alleys," *Washington Post*, March 24, 1956; "Zoners Ban All Building in Narrow D.C. Alleys," *Washington Post*, May 19, 1956.

40. "Controversial Alley Homes Completed," *Washington Post*, December 29, 1956.

41. "West Lane Keys Development: Georgetown Residents Lose Round in Fight against Dwelling Project," *Washington Post*, September 28, 1957.

42. Ad for West Lane Keys house in the *Washington Post*, January 18, 1959.

43. Richard Longstreth, "Brave New World: Southwest Washington and the Promise of Urban Renewal," in *Housing Washington: Two Centuries of Residential Development and Planning in the National Capital Area*, ed. Richard Longstreth, 255–80 (Chicago: Center for American Places, Columbia College, 2010); Keith Melder, "Southwest Washington: Where History Stopped," in *Washington at Home: An Illustrated History of Neighborhoods in the Nation's Capital*, 2nd ed., ed. Kathryn Schneider Smith, 88–104 (Baltimore: Johns Hopkins University Press, 2010).
Kirsten Downey, "1954 Court Case Opened the Door for Urban Renewal," *Washington Post*, May 7, 2005; Dean Madsen, "The Hidden History of D.C.'s Alleyways," DCist, December 26, 2018, https://dcist.com/story/18/12/26/the-hidden-history -of-d-c-s-alleyways/.

44. Wes Barthelmes, "First Walls in Squalid Dixon Court Pulled Down," *Washington Post*, April 27, 1954.

Chapter 5: Commerce and Industry in the Alleys

1. "Bread for a Whole City: A Wonderful Big Bakery and the Man Who Runs It," *Evening Star*, July 19, 1892. See also "Bakeshop to Bakery: Evolution of the Charles Schneider Company," *Evening Star*, December 16, 1902; and "Charles Schneider Dies Following Operation," *Evening Star*, July 27, 1911.

2. In 1910 the flats at 460 K Street NW housed twelve male employees, including two laborers, five drivers, a route manager, a bookkeeper, and the dairy engineer. National Register of Historic Places, "Mount Vernon Triangle Historic District," Washington, DC, 2006, no. 06000191.

3. Simpson's Walker Hill Dairy, advertisement, *Washington Times*, February 10, 1922.

4. *Washington Post*, December 22, 1912.

5. *Washington Post*, May 10, 1917.

6. "A War on Filthy Bakeries," *New York Times*, April 8, 1896.

7. National Register of Historic Places, "Dorsch's White Cross Bakery," Washington, DC, 2012, no. 11001076.

8. "New Home for Bakery Concern," *Evening Star*, August 21, 1915.

9. "Dorsch's Bread on Market for 30 Years," *Washington Post*, January 8, 1928.

10. According to the DC Historic Alley Buildings Survey (2014), approximately four hundred stable buildings survive in the city's alleys.

11. Jorrocks [pseud.], *The Private Stable: Its Establishment, Management, and Appointments* (Boston: Little, Brown, 1899), 54.

12. "The Embassy with a Dream House Past," *Washington Times*, January 22, 1987.

13. "B. F. McCaully, Proprietor of 'Tally Ho' Stables," *Sunday Herald*, February 22, 1891.

14. "The Leading Business Houses of the National Capital: Our Local Industries," *Washington Critic*, July 12, 1887.

15. "B. F. McCaully." Commercial liveries may have purchased their carriages from any one of several carriage makers in the city, such as G. W. Mason Wagon Works at the rear of 1074 Thomas Jefferson Street in Georgetown and William Walter's Son Carriage Company at 322 (Rear) Third Street NE on Capitol Hill.

16. "Wilbur Nash, Sr., 92, Retired DC Builder and Merchant, Dies," *Evening Star*, February 18, 1951.

17. "Fine Horses Once Gave Distinction to Capital," *Sunday Star*, March 31, 1935.

18. "Horses Burned Up," *Evening Star*, October 19, 1910.

19. Following the fire, the partially destroyed stable was repaired and converted into a box factory. A new apartment building that includes elements of the historic livery stable complex now occupies the site and is known as Chapman Stables. See National Register of Historic Places, "Chapman Coal Company Garage and Stable," Washington, DC, 2013, no. 13000845.

20. This information is based on the DC historic building permit database (DC Office of Planning / Historic Preservation Office), which records historical information from original building permits.

Chapter 6: Washington's Bohemia

1. "An Equestrian Statue: Innumerable Parts That Go to Make Up the Whole," *Washington Post*, August 4, 1895.

2. From 1791 to 1793, Andrew Ellicott surveyed the Territory of Columbia, first with African American astronomer Benjamin Banneker and later with his brothers Joseph and Benjamin Ellicott. Andrew Ellicott would complete the Plan of the City of Washington, designed by architect Pierre L'Enfant, after L'Enfant's dismissal in 1792.

3. Henry Ellicott had commissions up and down the East Coast, mostly for soldiers' monuments and equestrian statues of military figures and statesmen, but he maintained his studio in Washington, where he was one of the city's few resident sculptors. See "Our Local Artists; A Little Group That Is Growing Steadily Larger," *Evening Star*, December 9, 1893; and "The Cradle of Art: Artists Who Have Begun Their Careers in Washington," *Evening Star*, December 6, 1890.

4. "Henry J. Ellicott Buried," *Evening Times*, February 13, 1901.

5. National Register of Historic Places, "John Joseph Earley Office and Studio," Washington, DC, 2010, no. 117692106.

6. Earley's work can also be seen in Chicago at the Fountain of Time; in Wilmette, Illinois, at the Baha'i Temple of Light; and the Edison Memorial Tower in Menlo Park, New Jersey.

7. National Register of Historic Places, "John Joseph Earley Office and Studio."

8. "Flambeau Finds Washington's Bohemia in Hidden Haunt Where Cleon Throckmorton Stages His First Exhibition," *Washington Times*, February 5, 1922.

9. "Flambeau Finds Washington's Bohemia."

10. In 1919, in his early twenties and with little formal training, Cleon Throckmorton had two paintings selected for the Corcoran Gallery's seventh exhibition of contemporary American artists. Three years later, the Arts Club of Washington hung a one-man show of Throckmorton's work. Established by a group of

Washington artists in 1916, the Arts Club was inspired by London's Chelsea Arts Club and the National Arts Club in Manhattan. Its focus on art was an alternative to the city's more traditional social clubs. The Arts Club survives today as an art gallery, a site for performances and programs, and an elegant gathering place for members and their guests.

11. "Has Washington Genuine Art Colony, Asks Scientist," *Washington Herald*, July 31, 1921.

12. "Has Washington Genuine Art Colony."

13. "That Greenwich Village Shop," *Washington Herald*, February 23, 1920.

14. "Has Washington Genuine Art Colony."

15. "Has Washington Genuine Art Colony."

16. "Has Washington Genuine Art Colony."

17. Obituary of Mrs. Nelson Miles, *Evening Star*, August 2, 1904.

18. *Evening Star*, May 10, 1908; Iron Gate Restaurant menu, from the General Federation of Women's Clubs archives, unpublished.

19. When the General Federation of Women's Clubs prepared for opening its tearoom in the former stables in 1922, the club reached out to General Miles to learn the names of his horses stabled there. As reported in the *Evening Star*, "years had elapsed, but the general's memory had not faded. When he was asked to name the horses, he said without hesitation that they were Golden Pebbles, Denver, and General Wool. Those are now the titles of the booths." *Evening Star*, May 25, 1922.

20. Daisy Krier, "Artistic Tea Room Once Housed Horses of Gen. Nelson Miles," *Washington Post*, April 20, 1924.

21. "D.C. Greenwich Village Springs Up in Alley Once Home of Cattle," *Washington Times*, April 24, 1921. The article wrongly asserts that Zolnay's studio was "once home to cattle." It was, rather, a carriage house and stable.

22. "D.C. Greenwich Village Springs Up."

23. "In Exact Model: Nashville to Have Perfect Reproduction of Parthenon," *Chicago Eagle*, November 7, 1921; "'America Is Too Conventional to Appreciate the Nude' Says Zolnay, Capital Sculptor of Noted Achievements," *Washington Times*, May 14, 1922.

24. The *Evening Star* reported on October 31, 1920, that Catherine Critcher, who had been away for the summer, had resumed her art classes for indoor drawing and painting and out-of-door sketching and reopened her studio at 3 St. Matthew's Court, where "at present is an excellent portrait, not quite finished, of Mr. Zolnay, the well-known sculptor, who is her studio neighbor, and the first to remodel one of these studio-garages for studio purposes." See the *Washington Herald*, April 23, 1922.

25. "D.C. Greenwich Village Springs Up."

26. Virginia Lee Warren, "St. Matthew's Court Is City's Latin Quarter," *Washington Post*, November 7, 1934.

27. Warren.

28. Brian Brown's artistic creations consisted largely of caricatures of movie stars and bigwigs on the walls of "half the bars and cafes in Washington." See "Capital's Bohemia Is Quaint and Peaceful in Contrast to New York and Paris Gaiety; St. Matthew's Court Is City's Latin Quarter," *Washington Post*, November 7, 1934.

29. "Bohemia by the Cathedral," *Washington Daily News*, February 22, 1957.

30. "Art Careers in an Old Coachhouse," *Sunday Star Pictorial Magazine*, August 15, 1948.

31. "Two-Artist Show," *Evening Star*, March 14, 1950; "Katherine Hobbs of the Studio Group Has a Solo Show of Her Own," *Evening Star*, September 4, 1949.

32. Harriet Griffiths, "Artist with an Affinity for Animals," *Evening Star*, October 16, 1960.

Chapter 7: Reimagining Alleys

1. Grady Clay, "The Alley Revisited," *Landscape Architecture Magazine* 87 (1997): 139–40.

2. Thomas Dougherty, "The American Alley: A Hidden Resource," Strong Towns, 2001, https://static1.squarespace.com/static/53dd6676e4b0fedfbc26ea91/t/612016b8da04c87ea78656af/1629492930799/American+Alleys+e-book.pdf.

3. Michael David Martin, "The Case for Residential Back-Alleys: A North American Perspective," *Journal of Housing and the Built Environment* 17 (2002): 145–71.

4. Lindsey Layton, "Alley Homes Fight for Respect— and Trash Pickup," *Washington Post*, May 29, 2006.

BIBLIOGRAPHY

"Activities of the Arts Club of Washington." *Art and Archaeology* 12, no. 2 (August 1921): 85–93.

"Alley Dwelling Authority." *Federal Architect*, October 1938, 23.

Asch, Chris Meyers, and George Derek Musgrove. *Chocolate City: A History of Race and Democracy in the Nation's Capital.* Chapel Hill: University of North Carolina Press, 2017.

Associated Charities of Washington, D.C. Annual Reports, 1882–1935. Special Collections of the University Libraries at the Catholic University of America, Family and Child Services of Washington, DC, collection 43.

Beasley, Ellen. *The Alleys and Back Buildings of Galveston: An Architectural and Social History.* Houston: Rice University Press, 1996.

Bicknell, Grace Vawter. *The Inhabited Alleys of Washington, D.C.* Washington, DC: Committee on Housing, Woman's Welfare Department, National Civic Federation, 1912.

Borchert, James. "Alley Landscapes of Washington." *Landscape* 23, no. 3 (1979): 281–91.

———. "Alley Life in Washington: An Analysis of 600 Photographs." *Records of the Columbia Historical Society*, 49 (1973–74): 244–59.

———. *Alley Life in Washington: Family, Community, Religion and Folklife in the City, 1850–1970.* Urbana: University of Illinois Press, 1980.

———. "Builders and Owners of Alley Dwellings in Washington, D.C., 1877–1892." *Records of the Columbia Historical Society* 50 (1980): 345–58.

———. "The Rise and Fall of Washington's Inhabited Alleys." *Records of the Columbia Historical Society*, (1971–72): 267–88.

Brown, Letitia. "Residence Patterns of Negroes in the District of Columbia, 1800–1860." *Records of the Columbia Historical Society*, (1969–70): 66–79.

Clay, Grady. "The Alley Revisited." *Landscape Architecture Magazine* 87 (1997): 139–40.

———. *Alleys: A Hidden Resource.* Louisville, KY: Grady Clay, 1978.

Cromwell, Mary E. "The Human Side of a 'Washington Alley." Unpublished report for the Associated Charities of Washington, D.C., May 1915.

de Graffenried, Mary Clare. "Typical Alley Houses in Washington, D.C." *Women's Anthropological Society Bulletin*, no. 7 (1897).

Dougherty, Thomas. "The American Alley: A Hidden Resource." Strong Towns, 2001. https://static1

.squarespace.com/static/53dd6676e4b0fedfbc26ea91/t
/612016b8da04c87ea78656af/1629492930799/American
+Alleys+e-book.pdf.

Emenhiser, Bethany Mae. "Hidden Communities:
Creating a Preservation Plan for Underutilized
Alleyways as a Tool for Reactivation." Master's thesis,
Savannah College of Art and Design, 2015.

Faehtz, E. F. M., and F. W. Pratt. *Real Estate Directory of
the City of Washington*. Washington, DC: Faehtz & Pratt,
1874.

Fitzpatrick, Sandra, and Maria R. Goodwin. *The Guide
to Black Washington: Places and Events of Historical and
Cultural Significance in the Nation's Capital.* Rev. ed. New
York: Hippocrene Books, 2001.

Frankel, Godfrey, and Laura Goldstein. *In the Alleys:
Kids in the Shadow of the Capitol.* Washington, DC:
Smithsonian Institution Press, 1995.

Goode, James. *The Outdoor Sculpture of Washington, D.C.:
A Comprehensive Historical Guide.* Washington, DC:
Smithsonian Institution Press, 1974.

Green, Constance McLaughlin. *Washington: Capital City,
1879–1950.* Princeton, NJ: Princeton University Press,
1963.

Groves, Paul A. "The Development of a Black Residential
Community in Southwest Washington: 1860–1897."
*Records of the Columbia Historical Society, Washington,
D.C.* 49 (1973–74).

———. "The 'Hidden' Population of Washington Alley
Dwellers in the Late Nineteenth Century." *Professional
Geographer* 26, no. 3 (August 1974): 270–76.

Hage, Sarah. "Alleys: Negotiating Identity in Traditional,
Urban and New Urban Communities." Master's thesis,
University of Massachusetts, 2008.

Hannold, Elizabeth, "'Comfort and Respectability':
Washington's Philanthropic Housing Movement."
Washington History 4 (Fall 1992 / Winter 1993): 20–39.

———. "The Influence of Sanitary Housing Cannot Be
Over Estimated." In Longstreth, *Housing Washington*,
133–57.

Hayward, Mary Ellen. *Baltimore's Alley Houses: Homes for
Working People since the 1780s.* Baltimore: Johns Hopkins
University Press, 2008.

Hoagland, Alison, K. "Nineteenth-Century Building
Regulations in Washington, D.C." *Records of the
Columbia Historical Society,* 52 (1989): 57–77.

Johnson, Amy. "Crooked and Narrow Streets." *Winterthur
Portfolio* 47, no. 1 (2013): 35–64.

Jones, Thomas Jesse. "The Alley Homes of Washington."
The Survey, 29 (1912–13): 67–69.

———. *Directory of Inhabited Alleys, Washington, D.C.*
Washington, DC: Housing Committee Monday
Evening Club, 1912.

Jones, William Henry. *The Housing of Negroes in
Washington, D.C.: A Study in Human Ecology.*
Washington, DC: Howard University Press, 1929.

Jorrocks [Robert Smith Surtees]. *The Private Stable; Its
Establishment, Management, and Appointments.* United
States: Little, Brown, 1899.

Kober, George M. *The History and Development of the
Housing Movement in Washington, D.C.* Washington,
DC: Washington Sanitary Improvement Company,
1897.

———. *Report on the Housing of the Laboring Classes in the
City of Washington, D.C.* Washington, DC: Government
Printing Office, 1900.

Lesko, Kathleen M., Valerie Babb, and Carroll R. Gibbs.
*Black Georgetown Remembered: A History of Its Black
Community from the Founding of "The Town of George" in
1751 to the Present Day.* Washington, DC: Georgetown
University Press, 1991.

Lewis, Tom. *Washington: A History of Our National City.*
New York: Basic Books, 2015.

Logan, John R. "Racial Segregation in Postbellum Southern Cities: The Case of Washington, D.C." *Demographic Research* 36 (2017): 1759–84.

Longstreth, Richard. "Brave New World: Southwest Washington and the Promise of Urban Renewal." In Longstreth, *Housing Washington*, 255–80.

———. *Housing Washington*. Chicago: Center for American Places, Columbia College, 2010.

Mallalieu, Wilbur Vincent. "A Washington Alley." *The Survey* 29 (October 19, 1912): 69–71.

Martin, Michael. "The Case for Residential Back-Alleys: A North American Perspective." *Journal of Housing and the Built Environment* 17 (2002): 145–71.

———. "Endangered Landscapes: Residential Alley Transformations." *APT Bulletin: The Journal of Preservation Technology* 31, no. 4 (2000): 39–45.

Melder, Keith. "Southwest Washington." In *Washington at Home: An Illustrated History of Neighborhoods in the Nation's Capital*, 2nd ed., edited by Kathryn Schneider Smith, 88–104. Baltimore: Johns Hopkins University Press, 2010.

National Capital Housing Authority. *Report of the National Capital Housing Authority for the Ten-Year Period 1934–1944*. Washington, DC: Government Printing Office.

National Register of Historic Places. "Blagden Alley / Naylor Court Historic District." Washington, DC, 1990, no. 90001734.

———. "Chapman Coal Company Garage and Stable." Washington, DC, 2013, no. 13000845.

———. "Dorsch's White Cross Bakery." Washington, DC, 2012, no. 11001076.

———. "John Joseph Earley Office and Studio." Washington, DC, 2010, no. 117692106.

———. "Mount Vernon Triangle Historic District." Washington, DC, 2006, no. 06000191.

———. "Spencer Stable." Washington, DC, 1996, no. 96000894.

———. "St. James Mutual Homes." Washington, DC, 2016, no. 16000027.

———. "W. H. Penland & Company Stable." Washington, DC, 1994, no. 94001510.

———. "Walsh Stable." Washington, DC, 1986, no. 117692602.

Peatross, Ford, ed. *Capital Drawings: Architectural Designs for Washington, D.C., from the Library of Congress*. Baltimore: Johns Hopkins University Press, 2005.

President's Homes Commission. *Reports of the President's Homes Commission Appointed by President Theodore Roosevelt*. Washington, DC: President's Home Commission, 1908.

Ratigan, Marion. *A Sociological Survey of Disease in Four Alleys in the National Capital*. Washington, DC: Catholic University of America Press, 1946.

Reiff, Daniel D. *Washington Architecture, 1791–1861: Problems in Development*. Washington, DC: US Commission of Fine Arts, 1971.

Report of Commissioners of the District of Columbia for the Year Ended 1897. Vol. 1. Washington, DC: Government Printing Office, 1897.

Report of the Alley Dwelling Authority for the District of Columbia for the Fiscal Years 1934, 1936–44. Washington, DC: Government Printing Office, n.d.

Scott, Pamela, and Antoinette Lee. *Buildings of the District of Columbia*. New York: Oxford University Press, 1993.

Smith, Kathryn Schneider. *Port Town to Urban Neighborhood: The Georgetown Waterfront of Washington, D.C., 1880–1920*. Center for Washington Area Studies, George Washington University. Dubuque, IA: Kendall/Hunt, 1989.

Summer, Rebecca. "Comparing Mid-Century Historic Preservation and Urban Renewal through Washington,

DC's Alley Dwellings." *Journal of Planning History* 21, no. 2 (2021): 107–32.

———. "Stories of Change Hidden in Washington, D.C.'s Alleys." *American Association of Geographers* (blog), September 1, 2018, https://www.aag.org/author/rebecca -summer/.

———. "The Urban Alley: A Hidden Landscape of Social Change in Washington, D.C." PhD diss., University of Wisconsin, 2019.

Swinney, Daniel D. "Alley Dwellings and Housing Reform in the District of Columbia." PhD diss., University of Chicago, 1938.

———. "Washington: A City of Beauty and a City of Slums; Summary of a Thesis—'Alley Dwellings and Housing Reform in the District of Columbia.'" Washington, DC: Washington Housing Association, 1938.

Swope, Carolyn. "The Problematic Role of Public Health in Washington, D.C.'s Urban Renewal." *Public Health Reports* 133, no. 6 (2018): 707–14.

Tyler, Ilene R. "Replicating the John J. Earley Concrete Mix to Restore the Nashville Parthenon." *APT Bulletin: The Journal of Preservation Technology* 35 (2004): 43–50.

Weller, Charles F. *Neglected Neighbors: Stories of Life in the Alleys, Tenements and Shanties of the Nation's Capital.* Philadelphia: John C. Winston, 1909.

Williams, Kim Prothro. "D.C. Historic Alley Buildings Survey." Unpublished report, Historic Preservation Office, District of Columbia, 2014.

———. "The Surviving Cultural Landscape of Washington's Alleys." *Washington History* 27, no. 2 (Fall 2015): 40–52.

Wood, Edith Elmer. "Four Washington Alleys: Some Phases of Life in Fenton Place, Madison Alley, Essex Court and Naylor's Court as Brought Out in a Recent Survey." *The Survey* 31 (December 6, 1913): 250–52.

———. *The Housing of the Unskilled Wage Earner: America's Next Problem.* New York: Macmillan, 1919.

Zolnay, George Julian. "The Reconstruction of the Nashville Parthenon." *Art and Archaeology* 22, no. 2 (August 1921): 75–81.

INDEX

Note: Illustrations are indicated by page numbers in *italics*.

ABOUT THE AUTHOR

Kim Prothro Williams is an architectural historian who has been researching and writing about historic places and communities in and around Washington, DC, for the past thirty years. Since 2010 Williams has served as the National Register coordinator at the DC Historic Preservation Office, where her primary focus is on researching, evaluating, and documenting properties for listing in the National Register. In that process, she has studied a diverse range of buildings and communities and has developed a particular interest in the history of planning and the evolution of place. She enjoys discovering physical remnants of the past that reveal the transformation of their environments and that contribute to telling the stories behind the making of place. Williams is the author of many neighborhood history and heritage trail brochures, websites, blog posts, and articles dealing with the built environment and is the author of several books, including *Lost Farms and Estates of Washington, DC* (2018), *A Pride of Place: Rural Residences of Fauquier County, Virginia* (2003), and *Chevy Chase: A Home Suburb for the Nation's Capital* (1998).